The Corporate Director

The Corporate Director

New Roles ⎯•⎯ New Responsibilities

A Report of The Corporate Directors Conference

Produced by

**Arthur D. Little, Inc./Learning Systems
and the New York Management Center**

Published by

CBI Publishing Company, Inc.

51 Sleeper Street, Boston, Massachusetts 02210

Library of Congress Cataloging in Publication Data

```
Corporate Directors Conference, Washington, D. C., 1974.
   The corporate director : new roles-new responsibili-
ties.

   1.  Directors of Corporations--United States--Con-
gresses.  I.  Little (Arthur D.) inc.  Learning Systems.
II.  New York Management Center.  III.  Title.
HD2745.C63  1974        658.4'2      75-4838
ISBN 0-8436-0739-4
```


Library of Congress Catalog Card Number: 75-4838
ISBN: 0-8436-0739-4

Arthur D. Little, Inc./Learning Systems
15 Acorn Park, Cambridge, Massachusetts 02140

CBI Publishing Company, Inc.
51 Sleeper Street, Boston, Massachusetts 02210

Design and composition by Jay's Publishers Services, Inc.
Printed in the United States of America by The Alpine Press, Inc.

Fourth Printing

Contents

The Corporate Director

Welcome

Robert K. Mueller

Arthur D. Little, Inc.
Program Chairman and Moderator

Mr. Mueller, Vice President of Arthur D. Little, Inc., is Chairman of the Board of ADL International, Inc. and a Director of ADL, Ltd. (London). His work at ADL involves board of director and management aspects of multinational institutions; business development, new ventures, acquisitions, corporate planning, venture capital, and diversification in various industries and financial organizations.

Prior to joining ADL in 1968, Mr. Mueller was Vice President and a Director of Monsanto Company. He also served as Shawinigan Resins Corporation's President and Chairman of the Board. Together with numerous other business and professional affiliations, Mr. Mueller is a member of the Board of Directors of Massachusetts Mutual Life Insurance Company, Baystate Corporation, and Mass Mutual Income Investors, Inc.

Our work at Arthur D. Little is for an international clientele and we routinely concern ourselves with issues of complexity, uncertainty, and turbulence. In defining this conference there were two appeals that particularly intrigued us.

First, it was ADL's primary interest in the process of change, and all of the forces that are presently at work on the directorate. The second appeal is the analysis of the leadership role played by regents, trustees, and directors.

Many of us tend to view the directorate as a sacrosanct part of society—private and closed—but lately this notion has been challenged by shareholders, consumers, employees, managers, and even directors themselves. That is why we are here today.

As a result of these challenges, directors are sometimes caught in a cross-fire. Increasing potential liability and restraints on freedom become realities, but despite them the board room represents the pinnacle of achievement for many. The conditions of memberships on boards are toughening, and this is to everyone's long-term interest. One of the clearest challenges that we perceive at ADL is the challenge to the integrity and effectiveness of institutions, and the directorate is a particularly vulnerable part of this system.

I suggest that our directorate *system* may be out of phase with the real situation facing trustees, so, in designing this conference, we were careful to see that we represented both sides of the question. In introducing the subject, I'd like to make the first point: that a fundamental virtue of a board of directors lies not in its being expert in institutional affairs, but in having a sound and separate perspective to them. This perspective must be an informed and current one.

Introduction:
The Reshaping
of the Seventies

James M. Gavin
Chairman of the Board
Arthur D. Little, Inc.

James M. Gavin is Chairman of the Board of Arthur D. Little, Inc. He joined the company in 1958 following his retirement as Lt. General, after thirty-three years' service in the U.S. Army. A year after Mr. Gavin joined Arthur D. Little, Inc., he was named Executive Vice President and a member of the Company's Board of Directors. He was elected President in March 1960 and became Chairman of the Board in March 1964.

Early in 1961 he was named United States Ambassador to France by President Kennedy and served in that capacity until the fall of 1962, when he returned to Arthur D. Little, Inc. Mr. Gavin is a member of the Board of Directors of the John Hancock Mutual Life Insurance Company, the New England Merchants National Bank, and the American Electric Power Company, Inc.

When I joined Arthur D. Little 17 years ago, I was invited to join the board of directors and, shortly thereafter, the executive committee. I assumed at the time that I could go out to a bookstore and get a body of information about boards, about directors, about their responsibilities to shareholders, about their legal responsibilities, about the role of the chairman, and so on. There was nothing available.

Shortly thereafter, I joined the board of the American Light & Power Company and then the research committee of that board and, shortly thereafter, the executive committee of that board. Later, I joined the board of the New England Merchants National Bank and also of the John Hancock Mutual Life Insurance Company. I must say that it's been on-the-job training all the way. I hope that in bringing this body of expertise together here that we may bring forth a collection of information and guidance and wisdom for boards that will be very useful, and that has previously not been readily available.

I'd like to begin with a little story, if I may, of some of my past experience in the military establishment. Some years ago the military was facing some very difficult decisions. Those were the days before we had launched our first satellite. We had yet to launch a big missile, and we were still evaluating World War II. My colleagues in the

Pentagon—I was chief of R & D for four years—were continually thrusting upon me new ideas they thought were made possible by technology. The question was what to do, how to develop and how to fit it into the spectrum of human experience. Our problems were similar in form to those faced by Boards of Directors year in and year out.

It seemed to me that anything we did had to have some rational purpose to fit the learning experience of man in history. I spent a great deal of time studying anthropology. I learned one lesson from that experience which I hope you will not consider an overdrawn analogy to the business community. It is that in all the total experience in the life on earth, it has been the soft, fuzzy, intelligent, mentally-agile animal that has survived, not the animal that is protected against his environment by enormous shells about his head and shoulders, such as the triceratops and the dinosaur. They are long extinct.

I believe that the business community must see the challenges, of which there are so many now, as something to which they must respond with agility and imagination.

Now, I chose this subject, "The Reshaping of the Seventies," to permit me to talk about what we might do in the seventies that would lead us into the eighties and then beyond. I'd like to deal with this subject by discussing significant trends that are now discernible that will impact inescapably upon corporate life and thus upon the corporate board room.

First, the resources problem. A few years ago under the sponsorship of the Club of Rome, Dennis Meadows of MIT and his colleagues prepared a report published under the title *The Limits of Growth*. It had considerable worldwide impact. Projections made were not intended to be prophetic, but they were quite pessimistic. This pessimism stemmed directly from the assumptions on which the study was based.

The study served a very useful purpose. It caused many people to be concerned about the finite character of the earth's resources and the alarming growth rate of the earth's population. Many of these resource statistics are now under revision. One figure, however, persists in its validity. That is that world population will double by the year 2000.

The implications of this to governments and industries and to you as board members and officers are simply tremendous. Recently, a group of economists at the University of Amsterdam pointed out that it had taken centuries to provide housing, schools, and agricultural distribution for the existing population. The challenge of doubling this infrastructure in the next 25 years is immense, if not beyond the ability of man to respond adequately through his state and corporate organizations.

Today, another similar study on the global resources problem is being conducted for the United Nations under the leadership of Prof. Wassily Leontief. I recently talked with him about his tentative conclusions. Using input-output techniques, for which he received the Nobel Prize last year, he has been developing a model of the world situation for the year 2000. His conclusions are significantly more optimistic than those of *The Limits of Growth*. It is quite clear now that governments and industries and business will make every effort to adjust to the changing global environmental problems and resources problem on the almost day-to-day basis, and that success in doing this is possible.

The earth is an interplanetary body that can only carry so many passengers and it has only the support resources for this number of passengers. Population control, recycling, recovery of wastes, and the use of substitutes must become commonplace.

Clean air and clean water must become the concern of every corporation as well as every nation. These matters should impact on the thinking of every board room today. They will become of critical importance in the years that lie ahead. It is difficult to imagine any significant decision being made by a board that will not be affected to an increasing extent by the resources problem.

The international markets, in particular, as a reflection of the international political situation, are changing with surprising rapidity. The world in which we will be doing business in the seventies and into the eighties will certainly be one of very rapid change. Only yesterday we thought we were living in a bi-polar world. Nations were considered to be Communist or non-Communist, and others were considered to be in between, but they would be pushed inexorably toward these poles. Indeed, it was this view of the nature of the world that caused us to drift into the Southeast Asian War. As the thinking then went, we stopped Communism in Europe, we stopped it on the 38th Parallel in Korea, and now we were going to stop it on the 17th Parallel in Vietnam. But while many were preoccupied with this state of affairs, change was taking place, nationalism was emerging as a more dominant force.

I remember at that time attending an annual meeting given by *Fortune Magazine*. Its editor, who had just returned from a trip around the world, remarked at that meeting: "Remember, gentlemen, there are two blocks of power on this world. They are not going to change. They are going to, if anything, solidify in their particular spheres of interest." He was talking about the bi-polar world.

A few years ago, when he was a White House advisor, Secretary of State Kissinger enunciated with some of his colleagues in Harvard a view of the *five*-power world. The five powers were the Soviet Union, Red China, the European Economic Community, Japan, and the United States. What impresses me about this shift in global politics is that even the five-power concept is obviously no longer valid. But to understand where we are, a word about each might be in order.

The Soviet Union possesses tremendous national resources and a highly centralized government managed by the Communist Party. Despite its tremendous endeavors in the past 50 years, it has not achieved the high level of industrial production known to the West, nor has it been able to solve its management problems.

At the present time it is very aggressively seeking trade with the West through a policy of *detente*. The Soviets, of course, are motivated by self-interest. Not only do they want technological and management know-how from the West, they want to know that close trade ties with the West do exist, for they look with great apprehension upon their colossal neighbor to the east, Red China.

Relations between Red China and the Soviet Union are tenuous at best. The Red Chinese are exasperating to the Soviets. As the Chinese repeatedly remind the Soviets, Lenin said that the treaties entered into by the Czars and the Chinese warlords that resulted in the Czars' adding enormous areas of land to their holdings in Siberia, are null and void and should be abrogated. The Chinese are determined that this shall be done. In the meantime they maintain sizeable military forces on the Sino-Soviet Border.

I believe the Chinese would like to trade with the United States, but certainly any significant volume of trade is a long way off. Most of their efforts today are directed to caring, feeding, and educating a population approaching 800 million people. This, the present Red Chinese regime has accomplished with tremendous success. The Chinese will continue to watch our relations with the Soviet Union with unease and suspicion. They will also continue to work toward closer ties with us as the possibilities of such trade become more likely in the next decade, into the eighties.

The European Economic Community represents a tremendous economic force, but recently, its economy has come under very grave threats with its need for oil. France, for example, as many of you are well aware, has set an arbitrary quota of $10 billion that it will not exceed for any one year for the securing of oil. It is difficult to see how the European nations can solve their energy problem. Nevertheless, they are our oldest trading partners and will continue to be in the foreseeable future. With each passing year the nations of Europe and the United States will come closer together and increase their corporate ties.

Japan is a special case. Despite its military weakness, because of its great economic strength, it has been considered a great power. Indeed it was. The oil situation, however, has changed that completely. For the foreseeable future, the Japanese will depend heavily upon the oil-producing nations for the energy they need to support their own economy. But I really have a very deep conviction that we should never underestimate the resilience, industry, and durability of these very resourceful people. We should encourage and continue to build business ties with the Japanese.

Now, at the time of the enunciation of the five-power world, I was very struck by the fact that neither South America nor Africa was considered. Both of these vast land areas will, in the immediate future, because of their resources, be of increasing importance to the more developed nations. It may well be that the South American area could become one of the major powers on the earth. It should behoove us to cultivate business ties with South America and with Africa.

Looking back on the five-power world concept, it is obvious now that there are three major power blocks that should be added to the five: South America, Africa, and the oil-producing powers. However, there is no reason at all to believe that this power alignment will remain undisturbed. In fact, it is almost certain that within the next decade some nations that we now consider to be economic powers will deteriorate seriously, while others will emerge to challenge the global business community.

The key to understanding the business world of the foreseeable future is change. Change will be pervasive, sometimes unexpected; but it is our job as managers and directors to anticipate and be prepared to deal with it.

Massive changes also are taking place in world attitudes toward the transnational corporation. These will have significant impact upon the board room.

At the time that the Allende government in Chile was in existence, an action was initiated in the United Nations leading to an examination of the conduct of multinational corporations abroad. This examination was conducted by a working committee rather cumbersomely titled, "A Group of Eminent Persons to Study the Role of the Multinational Corporations on Development and on International Relations."

Recently, it recommended to the Economic and Social Council of the United Nations the establishment of an intergovernmental commission on transnational corporations. It is anticipated that the commission will recommend some form of code that would regulate behavior of transnational corporations. Admittedly, this would be a very difficult undertaking since every nation has its own ideas about how it would control corporate behavior. Nevertheless, it is a trend in the United Nations that is of great importance and should be followed very closely.

If this matter is brought before the General Assembly, the present voting pattern in that body would suggest that the advanced industrial nations may expect to find excessive restraints placed upon them and upon all their corporate activities in doing business abroad. Obviously, these trends should be followed closely and corporations should consider with great care their relations with host governments.

Now, this trend is not an isolated incident. For some time now, on my visits to businessmen and governments in South America, I have encountered great resistance to the growth, power, and influence of transnational corporations. At a meeting of the Council of the Americas, where I am a Trustee, the Minister of the Economy of Chile talked about the political climate in his country. He stated that his country is neither leftist nor an extreme right-wing government. He understands, I believe, the role of the corporation and the need for outside capital.

However, he did emphasize his government's conviction that corporations doing business in Chile must have directors from Chile on their boards. He urged this for two reasons: so that boards would be kept informed of what was going on in his own country; and, so that Chilean directors could convey the goals and purposes of the corporation. He discussed the need for workers on boards; co-management he called it. He expressed the belief this was important in order that management might understand the workers' point of view. He went on to say when management does have such understanding, then the corporation will have good management.

As he finally expressed it, Chile wants things to take place that will be, number one, in the interest of the government; second, in the interest of the workers; and third, in the interest of the corporation. Now, this may all sound revolutionary, but it's the trend of the times in Latin America. I was surprised when the 70 distinguished senior businessmen present all applauded enthusiastically at this very candid exposition of the point of view of the Chilean government.

In another matter having to do with transnational corporations, this past April, at the Pugwash Conference, the subject of transfer of technology was considered. Transfer of technology is a catchy phrase. Yet new technology is really equity. It is something that a corporation owns. And I see no reason whatsoever for the arbitrary transfer of this new knowledge just for the sake of doing it. It is quite an unlikely event.

Nevertheless, the Pugwash Conference came to the conclusion in their long report that this should be done; technology should be transferred, albeit with restraint and with long-time compensation in return and so on. This report is important to the business community of the United States.

So far I have discussed the resources problem and the changing political world in which the transnational corporation must do business. I view both of these as major issues that will impact significantly on corporations and on corporation management in future years.

There is a third factor that is pervasive and deeply troublesome. For a variety of reasons, governments may be expected to take a close and increasing interest in corporate behavior, more than they have in the past.

For example, the need for affirmative action programs continues and grows. If there were any doubts about the importance of this subject, they certainly were dissipated when the American Telephone and Telegraph Company recently was directed by the Courts to upgrade 50,000 women and 6,600 minority group workers. It also agreed to hire 4,000 men for roles traditionally occupied by females, and finally agreed to pay some $50 million in compensation. While this decision was dramatic because of the size of the judgment, there were many other actions taken and more will come later. To be sure that boards are fully apprised of conditions within a corporation, some boards have established committees on social responsibility that report directly, bypassing management, to the board. Regardless of the method used, the problems must be dealt with realistically and as a matter of urgency within the board room.

In the past year there's been increasing movement in the direction of appointing financial audit committees. We now hear that the Securities and Exchange Commission would like to institutionalize these financial audit committees and compel them to prepare reports to be made available not only to the board, but directly to stockholders; and if the corporation board does not have a financial audit committee, then they want an explanation why they don't have one.

Now that we find ourselves sort of deeply involved in international business with an ever-changing set of rules and characterized by increasing complexity, the federal government will certainly continue to take an interest in the United States corporation abroad. There is, of course, the problem of to what extent petrodollars may be used to buy into American industry. This is one of the most important problems confronting the federal government in the future, and the solution of the problem will impact upon many corporations.

At the present time the corporations come into being and operate under authority derived from the states in which they have incorporated. In discussions about this matter there has been a discernible tendency, for a growing body of opinion, to contend that the federal government, not state government, should grant charters to corporations. In this manner a degree of uniformity could be achieved. State and Federal government would be dealing with corporate entities that are at least identical in their origins and by-laws. This would make uniform the corporate purpose, and the relationship the corporation should have with its workers, management, shareholders. It no doubt will address itself to the problems and rights and responsibilities of managers and directors.

One way, of course, of federalizing corporate behavior—but repugnant to our free enterprise system—is nationalization. While we abhor nationalization—and understandably so—if our depression continues over a protracted period of time, more corporations may get into serious trouble, and I presume they will not hesitate to go to the federal government for support, with implications that differ only slightly from nationalization.

Ours is a very competitive system. When business and industry try to manage so as to produce a better product, or a better service, at a lower price consistent with profit, they are probably managing very well. Management, in any event, is very much part of that process. When a corporation fails, there is clear indication of management failure. When a major corporation must turn to government for financial help, the government is entitled to, and indeed obliged to, conduct a searching examination of management before a loan is granted; otherwise, major corporations, as they approach a critical financial condition, become in fact quasi-federal corporations and behave accordingly, knowing that the federal government is there to assist them if the existing management fails to keep the corporation viable. In any event, this interest and intervention in corporate management is now very much part of corporate life and probably will continue to be, and to an increasing extent, through the seventies and into the eighties.

In summary, I stated earlier that the one word that describes the international business community and climate today is change. I will use the same word to describe our domestic business community and business climate. Writing about business conditions in the *Harvard Business Review* last spring, a member of the faculty at the Harvard Business School, George Cabot Lodge, wrote: "If we wait, confident of somehow muddling through, we lurch from crisis to crisis until large scale depression and disruption causes us to welcome the orderly retreat of dictatorship."

I mention this opinion merely to establish it as one point on the spectrum of national opinion. Personally, I am far more optimistic about the future of our business community and about business conditions through the seventies and into the eighties. I have worked with governments and with corporations all over the world, and on both sides of the Iron Curtain. In my opinion, American management today is the envy of the world. If one could characterize Americans today any place in the world, it would be that they are superb managers. Management techniques developed by the Americans are sought all over the world. Management schools patterned after the American business school system, and teaching American management methods, are now in being in many parts of the world, and there will be more. So I have not the slightest doubt about our management, our management methods, and our management tools.

We are facing a very challenging and, to me, in many respects, a very exciting resources problem. We are confronted with the need to understand and adjust rapidly to the changing business conditions in the world of international business. This does imply the need for an examination of how we conduct our business, how we manage, and how boards behave in the United States itself. Coping with this is a very exciting prospect.

A very short time ago a banker friend of mine, Walter Wriston, gave a talk in New York in which he chose the title, "Even the Future is Not What It Used To Be." No, it is not. It is far more exciting, it is far more demanding, and infinitely more challenging than anything we ever envisioned. I welcome whatever it will bring.

The Impact of Change on Directors

Dr. Courtney C. Brown

Columbia University

Dr. Courtney C. Brown is Dean Emeritus of the Columbia Graduate School of Business. Following World War II, he was associated with the Standard Oil Company (N.J.) where his duties included serving as Economist, Assistant to the Chairman of the Board, and as a Director of Esso Standard Oil Company. He became Dean of the Graduate School of Business in 1954. Since that date, he has additionally served as Professor of Business Policy, as Editor, Columbia Journal of World Business; *as Vice President in charge of the business affairs of the University; and as the Executive Director of the American Assembly.*

He is a member of the Executive Committee of the Board of Directors of the Borden Company, Union Pacific Railroad and Associated Dry Goods Corporation and a Director of Columbia Broadcasting System.

We have just heard a fascinating account of a world in change, and I would like to pick up where Jim Gavin has taken us in this world of changing resources, changing political alignments and structures, and changing levels of economic growth.

We are now faced with a period of slower growth, even though it is not a no-growth prospect. This undoubtedly means there is going to be a tightness in society, and we are going to have tensions ahead. This has major significance for the business community in the way we organize our corporations, including the board of directors. Let me describe these external changes as they impact the corporation.

We are all familiar with the debilitation of the cities and the communities in which the corporations live, and with the demands that are being made on corporations from the standpoint of the ecological preservation of our society. World politics is changing. I am much impressed with Jim's progression from the bi-polarized earth to the five-power-centered world to the eight-power-centered world, including as additions to the five: South America, Africa, and the oil-producing countries. I would especially emphasize his reference to South America.

I recall vividly that in the last war a major source of resources was the Western Hemisphere. I think the United States made a frightful mistake in diverting our attention from South America shortly after the war terminated. But over and above this matter of the extension of the power centers to eight, it seems to me that there is another groundswell of change which is occurring in the world today. The 19th Century was organized to bring in raw materials from material-producing countries to the industrial countries, and the terms of trade were all in favor of the industrial world; a condition that has prevailed until the recent present. That is changing. The terms of trade may be in the process of reversing, and it's not a very comfortable position for the industrial countries looking ahead.

The multi-national corporations have proved to be the most effective means of organizing the world's resources and maximizing the effectiveness of their processing and their distribution. If we are going to develop codes of conduct for them, let's be sure that we develop codes of conduct for both host countries and home countries as well. Also, let's insure that such codes are not going to be punitive against the multi-national corporation any more so than restrictive against the home countries and host countries.

But there is still another group of changes. The ones we have been talking about are external changes. There is another group of changes that are internal to the company, and they are uniquely the concern of executive management. I won't go into them in great detail because I am sure that this sophisticated audience is fully familiar with them. I will simply refer to them in passing.

The sheer size of the corporation, its geographical spread, is a major change that has occurred in the last quarter-century. Conglomerate corporations as well as corporations that have not developed in a conglomerate sense, have widely diverse activities. Technological changes are occurring more rapidly. There is obsolescence of new products. The life cycle is much shorter today, as all of you know. There are new methods of mathematical analysis for determining operating problems. The administrative structure of a corporation is changing. The old rigid pyramid is giving way gradually to a far more flexible and malleable internal structure. The assurance of supplies is going to increasingly demand the attention of executive management, in addition to pricing decisions and the development of markets.

Laws are changing rapidly, whether they be in the anti-trust field, pollution, labor law, or even relationships to direct controls. Then there is the whole host of problems related to capital budgets, operating budgets, the maintenance of financial strength, the supervision of the reliability of financial accounts, and the importance of developing and maintaining free flow of information both up and down within the organization, including to the board.

That is a package of internal concerns that could very adequately occupy the attention of the most effective executive. In fact, as Arjay Miller has said, the CEO's job is becoming too much for any one man to handle. He might have said man or woman. Let me pick up three or four quotes from a fascinating issue of *Business Week* last May 4, which was devoted to the chief executive officer. These are quotes by CEO's.

"The amount of work necessary to prepare yourself to keep informed about the political situation, and how investors are reacting, is terrific and it keeps getting bigger." Or, again, "The CEO has switched from long-term planner to a short-term thinker. It is easy to go from crisis to crisis and let long-term planning slip. It would be easy to spend all your life on external problems and not really get into how the organization is functioning."

These are not all quotes from the same man. They are different CEO's, and important names that you would recognize readily. "The corporate woods are filled with companies in trouble because the CEO was not minding the store. At a time when the CEO is already under pressure because the company he runs has grown so vast and the economy is so tumultuous, he is being told to take on a new major function, that of envoy from the corporation to the world at large. Yet it just isn't practical for the CEO to have a junior officer make those decisions by which a corporation affects society."

Now what does this mean to the board of directors? The search is on within the corporation for some form of divided responsibility, call it consensus management, that will not lower the corporation's capacity for effectiveness and efficiency.

But so much for the diagnosis. What about the prescription?

The prescription may involve some fairly radical things about how to restructure the relationships between the board and management and, indeed, about the organization of the board and the activities of board members. One way to go at the problem is to identify the points of initiative in the corporation. To me it seems the board of directors is the logical place to lodge the initiatives in the external areas of concern to make the corporation more responsive to the pressures from the kinds of changes that Jim Gavin described.

But I submit that the board today is not equipped and not capable of accepting that initiative. I think it must be first strengthened by clarifying its functions relative to those of management in the internal affairs of the company. I submit that management must keep the initiative with regard to its internal affairs and its management, but that the board of directors must deepen its involvement in those internal affairs and in their relationship with management.

I would suggest a catechism of four P's for board members relative to these internal affairs. I will not elaborate, as I want to keep these remarks brief. The four P's are policy, procedures, performance, and personnel.

How can the board effectively determine policy? There are a variety of ways. One I will mention very briefly: a five-year running tableau of where the company is going, expectations reduced to numbers, is a perfectly good way. It should be revised every six months or every year.

To me it is a mistake for the board to divest itself of interests in the procedures used by the company because the procedures will determine exactly who does what and how.

Performance should be reviewed in an orderly and regularized manner. I am afraid the typical board doesn't do that now as thoroughly and comprehensively as it should.

On the matter of personnel, of course, the chief executive officer must have people around him who are congenial and effective and with whom he can work. But the board, I submit, must take greater interest in the development of the personnel programs and the management training in the succession, including the chief executive officer down.

The present practice of boards, on the other hand, is largely advisory, with review of management-sponsored proposals and review of performance usually only from the standpoint of the total P & L and balance sheet. I think there has been a substantial amount of progress made in the development of greater participation, independence, and service on the board, but in my judgment the board will not be strong enough to take on the challenges that it must in the interest of business unless several things happen. I will list them by number.

First, its functions and responsibilities with respect to internal and external affairs must be clarified.

Secondly, a distinction must be developed between the officers of the Board and the officers of the company.

Third, the jobs of the chairman and the president must be distinguished and separately assigned. When we assign one man as both chairman of the board and president, there cannot fail to be confusion as to the functions of the board; and the man himself is never quite sure whether he is speaking as the chief executive officer of the board or the chief officer of the company.

Fourth, a careful and systematic organization and supervision of the work of the board must be undertaken by the chairman. In other words, the chairman must be a working officer of the board and in most cases a full-time working officer.

Fifth, board members must commit much more time. I do not believe that members of working boards should be a member of more than two or at most three boards, and they should represent a wider range of backgrounds than they do at present.

I do not believe in constituency representation at all. I think if we had a group of board members, each of whom had a separate constituency, we would have a political organization that would fail to achieve the kinds of purposes that would be in the interest of the corporation. But I do feel that there is a place for a wide range of backgrounds.

I would not make the chief executive officer subordinate to the chairman of the board. I would make him of equal status with the chairman of the board in the sense that he would report to the whole board and not to the chairman. This does not represent in my judgment a dichotomy that separates management from the board in the sense of abrasive relationships. I like the title of one of the papers that you will hear from Mr. Magee, the President of Arthur D. Little, a little later in the program, "Creative Tension between the Board and the CEO."

Boards should not be a friendly club that feels it is part of management and must, therefore, react with great reservation to any searching or even critical appraisal of a view or position taken by management.

The CEO and his colleagues should have the initiative in all matters relating to operations which should be checked by the board. The board should take the initiative in responding to external influences that bear upon the company, but the board in turn should be checked by management with respect to these matters because I know of no significant actions in the field of social responsibility that aren't going to cost money in the short-run; maybe in the long-run it will preserve the opportunity to make money. But a board that is unchecked by management in terms of costs of its public activities or its public responsibilities could go haywire.

Conversely, it is unfair to expect management, guided by bottom line calculus, to give full recognition to social responsibility beyond public statements. It is not a question of what is good for management or what is good for the board. It is what is good for the company and for the total world of business. A system of checks and balances between the board and management rather than one man rule applied by giving two hats to one man as chairman and CEO is, it seems to me, the way the corporation can most vigorously develop itself in years ahead.

Two hundred years ago it was generally thought that there should only be one head man in the matter of politics and government. The divine right of a king had dominated political thinking up to that time. The founding fathers were really more revolutionary than most of us realize. They exploded that political theory by distributing power among the legislative, executive, and judiciary branches of government.

It may be time to accept the principle of consensus management in the corporation, and divide powers between the legislative functions of the board and the executive functions of management.

Thank you.

Question: I will ask Gen. Gavin a question on the size of the board membership that would be necessary to bring the board perspective on the global forces that you talked about.

Gen. Gavin: Well, the size of the board, of course, depends upon what you expect of the board; what committees you organize on the board; and how many members you need to deal with the day-to-day problems you have, particularly if you are a global corporation. I have administrative actions that the board must act upon with some frequency, and thus I need a sizeable working group of directors readily available in the Greater Boston area.

I think this question may bear a bit upon the proposal of the Chilean minister when he said, "If you are going to work in Chile, you should have a Chilean director." Of course, when you are an international corporation, you can't have a director in every country in which you do business. That is out of the question. Now, there are ways to go about that. For example, I have organized a European Advisory Board consisting of representations from several countries over there. It seeks to give the country's business community a feeling that they are being represented and it also gives the corporation an entity to which it can refer questions about the European problem.

This hasn't worked too well, but it seems to be one way to go about it. You cannot get representation from every geographic segment or every political body on the planet, or from every other interested group. You simply have to decide what you want and need on the board. You need sufficient numbers and sufficient skills to deal with the problems the board must confront, and you need sufficient people in your general vicinity to have people to work on very short notice when problems come up.

Question: Dr. Brown, are you suggesting that boards have full-time non-paid officers, that is, non-paid directors who are not part of corporate management?

Dr. Brown: No, I am not recommending they have full-time non-paid members. I think I would have them all compensated more than they are now because I would expect a whole lot more from them; more time, more attention, more careful study and participation on board committees.

I would have only one member of the management team on the board, and that would be the chief executive officer. I think as men or women in the company achieve a position that would otherwise entitle them to board membership, I would make them a board member, but I would divest them of all operating responsibilities and terminate their status as officers of the company.

Question: Would these people then be full-time paid directors?

Dr. Brown: Not necessarily full-time, no. They would be more time-committed than now would be the case as directors, but they would be encouraged to accept board membership on other corporations and in other activities in the community.

Question: The chief executive officer, do you feel or favor that he come from internal sources—not the chief executive officer, the chairman?

Dr. Brown: The chief executive officer would undoubtedly come from internal sources, but would not necessarily then progress to chairman of the board. That's a different job. As a matter of fact, he might be far too valuable as the chief executive officer to make him chairman of the board. You might take your chairman of the board from within your company or you might take him from outside. It would depend entirely on the circumstances. But more likely he would be taken from inside.

But I would not make the chief executive officer subordinate to the chairman of the board. He would be the chief executive officer of the company, and the chairman of the board would be the chief executive officer of the board. The functions are different.

Gen. Gavin: We actually have that setup at the present time; it's been in being for a year in the case of ADL. The chief executive officer is John Magee. I am chairman of the board and he is chief executive officer.

Dr. Brown: Does he report to the full board and not to you?

Gen: Yes.

Dr. Brown: That's what I am recommending.

Question: Gen. Gavin, please comment on the military and military procurement impact you anticipate in the new economic world you describe as regards the board.

Gen. Gavin: Yes, this is a terribly important question and it deserves far more time in answering than I can give it here this morning. I wish I could get businessmen really interested in this so they understand what we are talking about when we discuss a $100 billion defense budget. You see, the parameters of what constitutes national power between nations and among nations are changing on a day-to-day basis. Today, all the hardware resources we have in being for tactical purposes, that is bombs, missiles, Tridents, B–1's, and so on, exist through engagement of Soviet counterparts. The dimensions of a national strategy, therefore, now have gone into a whole new order of magnitude.

It consists of the economy of the country, the domestic condition in the broader sense of that word, and the priorities to which we allocate resources to our future survival, that is search for new energy sources, and so on. Now, when we are spending a national defense budget for hardware approaching $100 billion or more at the expense of these other three things I have mentioned, we might be well on a future disaster course because the country could get into a very deep depression, very serious problems, and we would really be serving the interests of the Soviets.

I am extremely disturbed when we go to Vladivostok and reach agreement to achieve higher levels of defense spending when we have overkill on overkill on overkill in the existing hardware, and I am more disturbed when we say we are doing it because the Soviets are doing it. Gentlemen, we shouldn't do anything because the Soviets are doing it. We should be on the initiative of our own, doing the things we know to be sound, proper, and appropriate for the business community and for the society as well as the military establishment. Let the Soviet Union copy us.

Question: Dean Brown, your statement that you do not believe in constituency representatives on boards suggests that you reject representation from such groups or minorities as women, consumer representatives, for the sake of having such representation. Exactly what organizational relationship do you propose for the CEO and the chairman of the board?

Dr. Brown: I am grateful for that question because it gives me an opportunity to elaborate on what I really mean. I do not believe in constituency representation. That does not mean that I would feel it inappropriate or undesirable to have minority representation on boards or different backgrounds on boards. In fact, I urge it. But I feel that a board of directors must not become a parliamentary body with tradeoffs among members representing their unique and specific constituency, whether it is labor, whether it is minority blacks, whether it is women, whether it is a religious order.

I feel that board members must have their first loyalty to the total effort of the organization which they are serving. And I think the quality of their thinking and of their discussions will be enhanced by the presence of people with different backgrounds, some of whom may not have had very much business experience. But if they can relate their backgrounds to the interests of the organization, the corporation, it is a tremendously valuable addition to the deliberations of the board.

As to the relationship between the chairman and the CEO, I think the chairman of the board is the senior officer responsible for organizing and supervising the work of the board of directors, for seeing it is refreshed with new members, seeing that procedures are developed for the elimination of members who have passed their point of usefulness. His is the responsibility for the board.

The chief executive officer is exactly that, chief executive officer of the company's operations. He should not have his functions reporting to the chairman of the board. The chief executive officer would report to the whole board. He would not be junior to the chairman of the board. They would be men of equal status in the organization.

Question: Gen. Gavin, are there sufficient real incentives to provide for development which is oriented first to the interest of government, second to the interest of workers, and only last to the interest of the corporation?

Gen. Gavin: I have talked to Latin American ministers about this situation and it is quite fascinating to me. Of course, this is their view; it isn't our view, I am just saying this point of view exists and prevails in a very powerful way. I was intrigued talking to the Minister of Industrial Development of Peru about a year after the takeover from W. R. Grace of the plantations, sugar, rum, so on. They appointed a committee of delegates, a sizeable committee, to administer. They then had a subordinate financial committee and a management committee in parallel supervising. They sufficiently aroused the workers with the concept that it was *their* business that they started to increase production from then on. They took off and did very, very well.

They soon began to figure out that they were losing good technicians because they saw no future there in this kind of an operation and they began to drift to other countries. I mean trained technicians. They also realized slowly they weren't investing in the future in getting new equipment and automating and modernizing their production lines and so on. So they were pretty grim about their future prospects and they are trying to get far back in. Nevertheless, they were making the damn thing work.

I talked with the W. R. Grace people about it and they told me they had proposed a system something like this to the workers in the beginning, but they couldn't get them to buy it. What interested me was that we have American investments going back 25 years or longer in many of those countries. It is in our mutual interests to make this system work if this is the way they must make it work.

The Art of Choosing
Board Members
PART ONE

Robert E. Brooker

Marcor, Inc.

Robert E. Brooker is Chairman of the Executive Committees of Marcor Inc., and Montgomery Ward and Company. Mr. Brooker joined Montgomery Ward as President and then, in 1966, as Chairman of the Board and Chief Executive Officer, Mr. Brooker successfully engineered the "turn-around" that re-established Montgomery Ward as a growth-oriented, profitable enterprise. In 1968, he conceived and executed a merger with Container Corporation of America, to create Marcor, Inc., a new $2 billion-plus consumer- and marketing-oriented corporation.

Mr. Brooker is also on the Board of Directors of Container Corporation of America, CNA Income Shares, and Chicago & North Western Transportation Company.

In this day and age the process of selection of directors by professional management and nominating committees of the board, which are made up of outside directors who are usually professional managers also, is one to serve the needs of the company and the stockholders.

Basically, it is a long-range planning job which involves setting specifications of the kind of experience which is most useful to the business and finding that talent as needed. Usually vacancies occur on retirement of board members. However, with management changes, mergers, and takeovers, such restructuring of the board is much more abrupt.

Now, I am going to go through the case history of Montgomery Ward, its successor, the Marcor Corporation, and our new associate and 51 percent stockholder, Mobil. And I don't present this to you as a pattern for you to follow. I present it to you because I think each board has its own requirements and the nominating committee of the board and the management have to think through its problems and needs, and make up a similar set of specifications for the board members they require.

The present management of Ward and Marcor moved into the company at the end of 1964. At the time the management joined the company, it was agreed with the board that new talent was needed on the board. The company had suffered nine successive years of reduced earnings and was projecting a further reduction for that tenth year. The new management, in analyzing the short-term plans, felt the need of specific talents on the board during that period in which it planned to invade major markets with large retail stores, and where it expected that losses would be inevitable during the first three to five years in each market until it built a base to establish its services.

We knew that the earnings potential of the smaller stores and the secondary markets, which had sustained the company for many years during the past, had eroded beyond recovery during a long period where no capital went into new facilities or modernization and very little into maintenance. In addition to the problems with the small stores, the mail order had never actively promoted the sale of major appliances nor had they ever been aggressive about getting in the credit business. And the new management felt that in order to get the growth that it projected, it had to concentrate on both the durable goods and credit. Consequently, they felt that the board, who would be asked to support these programs, had to realize the financial consequences of the expansion, of the credit business, and of the change in direction.

We knew that the board would face a difficult period when the earnings, at best, would be flat and might even decline. And since they would be expected to approve the policies and capital programs, there had to be expertise on the board to evaluate management's proposal and to review performance against the previously established objectives. The store expansion program needed money beyond the projected retained earnings and the depreciation was minimal since there had been very little capital spending for the past 20 years. The expansion of the credit business would require large sums.

If we had known that our receivables would grow from under $200 million to $2 billion, I think we might have been appalled at the prospect. But at least we knew we needed financial talent that would appreciate these problems, and evaluate our programs and performance.

We also felt that we needed an economist along with this financial talent because our business was marginal and depended on incremental sales. We felt that if we had an economic downdraft, that we would have problems maintaining our program and might even have problems surviving. And if we had an outside economist on the board to review our timing of our programs and where we were going, it would be helpful to the board in total.

We knew we were going to have an internal economist, but it is good to have a double check at the board level. We knew that we needed marketing expertise, particularly in the area of durable goods. Our percentage of the appliance business through our sales was six percent. Our competitor was enjoying a 20 percent ratio of appliance business to total sales. So here was an immense opportunity if we could get into that business. So we needed marketing experience there, particularly.

We also needed expertise in the real estate and construction business. For the first time we were entering major markets with groups of stores, large stores. We had no internal expertise that would guide us except that expertise we attracted as we went in. And we knew that this expertise on the board would be most helpful. We did have some marketing talent on the board in Bill Millegan, who was president of Pure Oil Company, and he had a chain of marketing outlets that were very successful. And Bill stayed on the board and he served until his retirement.

Transportation costs were an important element in our cost of sales; four percent on incoming freight and two percent on distribution cost of sales. We had Ernie Marsh, chairman of Santa Fe, and he was a very valuable director and served until his retirement.

We had an internal director, Chuck Kuchelle, who is a financial man, and he was a very strong director and he was the one that, when he was turned loose, put us in the credit business. We knew it would be difficult to attract the talent we needed with the short-range prospects as dim as they were, but Ward had a fine name and we found qualified executives willing to join us and take the heat for a few years with us. We laid it on the line in talking with prospects. But we underestimated the turn-around time. I think perhaps our new directors discounted our optimism, but signed on anyway.

Having established these specifications of our needs, we added the following to our board: Elliott Bell, an economist and editor at that time of *Business Week*, and Donald Graham, chairman of Continental Illinois Bank of Chicago; both largely for their financial know-how, Elliott because of his economic background. We added Fairfax Cohn, then chairman of the advertising firm that he founded, Foote, Cohn, & Belding, not because we wanted agency talent, because all of our advertising is handled internally, but because of his market research know-how and ability to guide us on building customer acceptance and a better image.

We added James J. Nance, who had been sales manager of Frigidaire and later was president of Hotpoint, for his marketing expertise, and he had been in the automotive business in the interim. A year later we added Edward Gudeman when he retired as Undersecretary of Commerce. He had been merchandising vice president of Sears, Roebuck and a colleague of mine during that experience, and he was a very valuable member of the board.

And finally we added Dwight Cochran. He was president at that time of Curran County Land Company, but he had been president of Safeway Stores, and he brought us marketing know-how. Thus, we added four directors with good marketing backgrounds: Cohn, Nance, Gudeman, and Cochran; and two financially oriented people: Bell and Graham. In geographic distribution, which is important to us because of the spread of our outlets, we had two from New York, one from Cleveland, and one from California.

The merger with Container made it possible to consolidate talents and further strengthen the board. We added Gaylord Freeman, chairman of the First National Bank of Chicago, and another production-oriented executive in William Drake, chairman of Penwall Company in Philadelphia.

Over the years we have lost all of our original directors through retirement, but have replaced them with talents we sought originally. Our problems aren't as critical as they were in 1961, but the need for talent and expertise to assure the growth of the business is just as great. Let me name the replacements and their special talents. Dan Gelworth, a real estate development expert from Columbus, Ohio, experienced in the field of construction and financing of large office buildings and dwellings, has been able to make a substantial contribution to us in our capital planning.

Arthur Neilson, Jr., President of the best known market research company, is well oriented in consumer goods and the marketing trends in retail. Charles Brown was president of the Illinois Bell Telephone when we added him to our board in communications. He's since been promoted to executive vice president of AT&T in charge of their financial programs. And recently we found the talents we required on the board in both a woman and a member of the minorities. We felt this representation as important, if not more so, than the geographic representation that we had always sought.

We added Leonard Evans, publisher of *Tuesday,* a publication supplement used by major newspapers for distribution in predominantly black markets. Mr. Evans is black, he has had 25 years of marketing experience, and adds to that expertise in the company. We added Marina Whitman, professor of economics at the University of Pittsburgh, a member of the National Price Commission, and a member of the President's Council of Economic Advisors, here again filling in that economic slot.

I have given you our experience of selection of directors with specific talents to appraise management's recommendation and performance. Your needs, as I stated to begin with, will differ from ours, but by the same processes you can develop your own specifications. Our specifications were financial or investment, economic and market research, marketing, real estate and construction, production, and communication.

Attracting candidates should be the job of the chief executive of the company. If the chief executive has learned by serving on other boards that there are advantages in hearing and sharing problems and solutions, even though the businesses are totally different, he is in a much better position to attract another chief executive to join the board. All our top people serve on at least three to five boards, which is slightly above Courtney Brown's specification.

We assure the new director that the board is structured so that he can perform his duties without undue burden on his time. We do this by carefully structuring our board committees. The audit committee has specific requirements; they meet twice a year with the outside auditors. The nominating and compensation committee—two insiders, three outsiders—nominates the top officers, nominates the directors, and reviews all of the compensation programs of the company. On most of the compensation reviews that involve officers' compensation, the three outsiders are the committee.

The finance committee, which reviews the long-range needs and the programs, meets about quarterly, with the financially oriented people on the board. Our executive committee meets monthly, and this is a long meeting. It reviews the performance of each of the companies in detail. It is a screening committee; it screens any proposal that is going to come to the full board. While the executive committee has the authority to act for the board, very seldom do we call on the executive committee for that kind of action. We like to have the executive committee screen the proposal, prepare it in detail, send it to the full board at least a week or 10 days before a board meeting so they can familiarize themselves and come in prepared to discuss the recommendation of the executive committee.

We have five board meetings a year. No director on our board has missed more than one meeting in any one year and most of our directors are 100 percent in their attendance. And I think this is important to the stockholders when you have five meetings that they have this attention and they are at least at four or five of our meetings, so it does take time on that day.

Now, that's a case history of Montgomery Ward. We have just added four new directors from Mobil; since they have 51 percent of the stock that seemed like an appropriate recommendation to make. (Laughter.) I don't know whether that violates any of Courtney Brown's principles, but I think it is very practical.

The Art of Choosing Board Members

PART TWO

John H. Johnson

Johnson Publishing Company, Inc.

John H. Johnson is the founder of the publishing company which now publishes books and five magazines, including Ebony, Jet, Ebony, Jr., *and* Black Stars. *He is also Chairman and Chief Executive Officer of Supreme Life Insurance Company of America; Chairman of WJPC, Chicago's first and only black-owned radio station; and President of Fashion Fair Cosmetics.*

He is a member of the boards of several companies, including: Bell & Howell Company; the Greyhound Corporation; Arthur D. Little, Inc.; Marina City Bank; Service Federal Savings and Loan Association; Twentieth Century-Fox Film Corporation, and Zenith Radio Corporation.

I was elected to my first board by starting my own company. Which is one way to get on the board. My second board membership came because I bought more than 51 percent of another company, which is another way to get on the board. However, I think that now many people are getting on in ways other than buying and starting their own companies.

The board room door is open and I think we ought to know that the public is looking in. Public interest in the board room proceedings has grown rapidly over the past few years. More and more Americans are reading the financial pages and business journals in an effort to improve their economic literacy and to unravel the management mystique that surrounds the stewardship of our nation's economic resources. America has been to the moon. Its next giant step could well be into the board room.

Stockholders are demanding more information from annual reports these days. They are no longer satisfied with pretty pictures of the newest products or the chairman of the board on location at a new plant. Investors and the general public alike want hard-nosed information about where the corporation has been in the past year. They want to know where it is going, how it is going to get there, and who is going to take it there. It is almost useless to close the board room door since the walls are literally made of glass. The public is looking in on the board and it is to the best interests of the board to look out at the public.

The choice of directors has, therefore, become crucial in establishing and maintaining communication between the corporation and the public, which is so vital in our times. The perspective of the board of directors must be broadened through the wise election of qualified or qualifiable members. We add the words "qualifiable" primarily to blacks and women and other minorities because many times people say they are not qualified, and so we say perhaps they are not qualified, but they can be qualifiable. And one of the realities is that the public is growing increasingly concerned about the profits we make, how we make them, and what we do with the profits after we make them.

Boards of directors no longer just represent the interests of ownership exclusively. Whereas stockholders remain paramount among the constituencies of corporations, the contemporary need is also for broader representation in all board room decisions. In the past, stock ownership was most concentrated among a small number of people, a few private and professional investors and a few families. Each class of investor held a substantial number of the shares outstanding. Each board member had a personal stake in the enterprise and devoted a sizeable amount of time and attention to looking after the affairs of the corporation.

However, the boardroom now is no longer a sanctuary for private capital nor a millionaire's reserve. Today legal ownership of a corporation is widely held by millions of investors. The private business sector is becoming increasingly public in the light of our changing world economy, the energy shortage, and the impact of management decisions which affect the environment.

In the past few years we have witnessed a mounting effort to make boards of directors more representative of stockholders, environmentalists, consumers, and a sundry of social activists. I personally do not believe that boards of directors can and must reflect all of the racial, ethnic, and social attitudes within our society. This is neither practical nor feasible. But I do think it is in the corporation's best interests to have first-hand access to all the main currents of American life. The boards of directors must be a main line of communication, a source of advice, consultation, and information between the corporation and the public it serves.

I am extending my concept of the word "public" to mean more than just customers. A corporation's constituency is made up of far more than its customers. The art of choosing board members has, therefore, become a crucial executive function in corporate management and survival. The corporation's need for profits, continuity, and growth should be paramount in the criteria for board membership. But we must develop standards for corporate success that go beyond the profit making objective. I believe that maximization of profits is the mission of management, but I also believe that the rule of reason must prevail. The maximization of profits must take place in the interest of the public as well as the investors.

Profit making must not become profit taking. The age of the robber baron is dead. The public today is too enlightened. The maximization of profits and the conduct of business in the public interest can be made compatible and mutually supportive. If business fails to accomplish this, our system of free enterprise is in grave danger of foreclosure. Balancing the board is just as important as balancing the budget. In electing board members, we must be careful to balance inside or management-oriented directors with outside or public-oriented directors. The board room must never become a battleground for conflicting interests. The resulting conflict would stifle the creativity and initiative required to solve the many diverse problems faced by management today.

I believe that the qualifications for both the inside and outside directors should be essentially the same. The new board members should bring to the table some expertise, some experience, or some other human resource that is needed by the corporation. It is not enough to appoint men or women to a board of directors merely because they are black or rich or young or because they represent some strong power base in the corporation's operating environment. This is not to say that these people should be excluded, however.

The prospective board member should have a proven record of his own and an understanding of the problems that will face the corporation. Corporate stewardship is no game for the amateur. The game is real, the stakes are high, and the armchair reformer need not apply. I believe that a board member should have the time that it takes to do an effective job. In choosing a board member I would urge that we select someone who has the time as well as the talent to serve.

I would be the first to argue against the individual board member's right of dissent and intelligent debate. But I do think that a sense of loyalty to corporate objectives is essential for effective board participation. Once a decision has been reached through consensus or by clearcut majority, I think a board member should support it whether he agrees with it or not. If a director cannot accept a lawful decision or action made in the interests of the corporation, I think he should step down or be challenged for cause. And whereas I do not question the right of a person to serve on a board for reason of economic conviction, I do believe that a prospective board member should be supportive of our free enterprise system and of the profit incentive.

You can't run a railroad without tracks and you can't run a company for long without profits. A person whose economic persuasions are far out of line with the free enterprise system should not be elected to board membership. Why give a man a shovel to bury you with when you aren't even thinking of dying?

And lastly, I think that a prospective board member should be free of undue management influence. This is not to say that management opinion should not be solicited when needed. If a board cannot rely on the information it gets from management, it should get rid of the management. But the board members must not be subservient to or overly dependent upon management. Board members are not elected to serve management, but to serve the corporation. In fulfilling this trust, they advise and consent. I believe that a strong management needs a strong board and I also believe that the strong board needs to develop a strong management. Good management does not fear strong boards, but it profits from its evaluations and review functions.

Where does a corporation look for new directors? I strongly advise that our search go beyond talented top management and that we tap the vast reservoir of expertise historically neglected. Ten years ago, for example, there were no blacks on the boards of directors among the *Fortune* 500 U.S. corporations. Now there are still less than 100. This is a substantial increase from zero, and I would remind you that zero was once a quota.

But when you consider the fact that the nation's 1,000 largest corporations have a total of some 14,000 directors with less than 100 blacks, you can readily see that we have barely scratched the surface. We are a long way from the bottom of the barrel in tapping black executive and professional expertise qualified for board membership. We have been skimming the cream, but the milk can also provide nourishment.

There are thousands of qualified and qualifiable blacks with the intelligence, the knowledge, the energy, and the time to serve as corporate directors. We need only to look into our schools, our hospitals, our churches, our businesses, and other institutions to find them. There are black economists, lawyers, scientists, engineers, and educators just waiting to be tapped. What is needed is a stepped up executive search for these men and women. The black community has been neglected for so long that these highly competent people may not always be visible, but they can be found if the commitment to finding them is there; and we do have to have the commitment.

I recall that some years ago when we decided to integrate our staff with whites, you'd be surprised how many excuses our black employees found for not employing whites. I recall that the first white employee we had when it got around the office we were going to employ, a petition was going around in the office and they demanded a meeting with me. And they said, "We understand you are going to hire a white fellow." And I said, "Yes." They said, "Well, it's all right to hire him, but we don't think he ought to be in charge of anybody. We think you ought to start him at the bottom and make him work up the way they do us." Then they said, "We don't think he ought to sit in the front of the office," and they wanted to know where I would sit him. I said, "Well, we will sit him in the middle of the office." So there were all these questions.

And I recall that we wanted to employ whites in our New York office and our New York manager said he couldn't find any. He said, "You know, they are hard to find." "Many of them," he said, "are not qualified." And so there came a time when we were even about to be cited by one of the commissions in New York for discrimination because we had no white employees, so the manager called me up one day and he asked me, "What are we going to do about answering this complaint?" And I said, "Well, I am not going to do anything, but you are going to find some white people or I will find a new manager." And you'd be surprised how many qualified whites he found before it was time to answer that complaint.

I think in selecting a black director it is important that he be motivated to the same level of performance as the other members of the board. The black director brings to the board something other than a different skin color. Too often black directors are used only as consultants on matters pertaining to blacks. I think that this is a tremendous waste of talent and potential. A sense of belonging and a sense of pride in being a member of the Board is essential to all directors. But it is a very sensitive point with the black director.

The qualified black director who is worth his salt would be infuriated to learn that he was elected to the board to fulfill an affirmative action quota. The resident black has outlived his usefulness. The showcase black director serves no meaningful purpose of the board or the meaningful constituency from which he comes. The majority of black directors see themselves as representing the black community, but also as serving in a useful way in the corporation.

I think we should also think in terms of selecting more women, and we should select them not because they are women, but because they are qualified to do the same job that any other director can do. It is the duty of board members to put their diverse perspectives on the table and to familiarize themselves with the full range of issues that will come before them as directors. Once a director accepts trusteeship over a corporation, he must accept its struggle against other institutions and must also accept the interest of the total community as a higher order of attainment.

I am sure it is no news to you that the American public has lately been expressing a growing dissatisfaction with the management of our economy, and it is also no news to you that the public has laid this dissatisfaction at the doorstep of business. A recent study by Opinion Research Corporation points out that the public's growing criticism of profits reflects much more than just a growing rise in the cost of living. No longer does a majority of the American people believe that corporations should be allowed to make all the profits they can; and no longer do most of the people in this country ascribe to the idea that higher productivity alone is the best way to achieve a better life.

These are sound warnings for business to put its board room in order. A recent survey by the Lou Harris organization concluded that the degree of confidence in corporate management was at a very low ebb. The Harris survey pointed out that only 16 percent of Americans have confidence in the financial community. Only 19 percent of all stockholders considered stocks to have worthwhile liquidity value. And 60 percent of all stockholders considered stocks to be a luxury.

It is against a backdrop of damaged credibility that management faces new ownership. The board of directors is no longer engaged in activities that affect only its owners and managers. Policies forged in the board rooms affect a wide segment of our society. As the private business sector becomes increasingly public, the social and economic groups whose lives and fortunes are dependent upon it are demanding greater participation. Our increasing efforts to broaden the board perspective must, therefore, continue.

This will provide the corporation with a much needed window to the outside world. The corporate community, which has been largely responsible for giving this nation the highest standard of living in the history of the world, has the capability, I think, to right itself. Rather than having a sense of corporate responsibility imposed upon it by the government or some other outside institution, the corporation should heal itself in the American tradition.

To accomplish this task, my advice to the corporation is to open the board room doors even wider and to keep them open to all qualified and qualifiable persons.

The Art of Choosing

Board Members

PART THREE

Ralph F. Lewis

Harvard Business Review

Ralph F. Lewis is Editor and Publisher of the Harvard Business Review, *and has had a varied background in business, government and education. He has been an FBI agent, an Assistant Controller for* Time, Inc., *an Assistant Managing Editor for* Fortune, *and a Management Consultant with Booz Allen & Hamilton.*

Mr. Lewis is a Director of the Houghton Mifflin Company, the Tele-Promp-Ter Corporation, Paine, Webber, Jackson & Curtis, Inc., Twentieth Century-Fox Film Corporation, and Frank B. Hall & Co., Inc. He is a Member of the Board of Governors, Harvard Business School Association of Boston, The Board of Visitors, Boston University College of Business Administration, and a Member of the Corporation, Babson College.

The first topic in my remarks about choosing board members is who makes the selection of directors and how. What happens most frequently, as most of you probably know, is that the CEO decides on what is needed, he talks to friends—sometimes including board members—makes his selection, and then submits the slate to the board for approval.

What I'd like to recommend is what General Motors does, which is a full discussion with the board about the type of person desired. At that time a committee of outside directors selects candidates, and the CEO has the right of veto only. Then the board either approves or disapproves as a unit.

My second topic is the need for any inside directors except the CEO. In this case I agree with Courtney Brown and by inference, at least, I disagree with John Johnson. I don't see any reason that any company executive besides the CEO should be on the board of directors. The typical inside director is well aware of his or her relationship with the CEO and cannot be expected to do battle with the CEO in front of outsiders.

The presence of insiders may inhibit free discussion, particularly of performance problems. Also, company executives should not be put in the position of acting as both advocate and judge. I see one possible exception, and that is where the COO, chief operating officer, position exists. It is conceivable to me that he might sit on the board so that he gets a real flavor of what the board discussion has been.

Next, I'd like to talk about untapped sources of director candidates. I have five areas that I think have not been sufficiently mined. One of these are the practical academics, including business school professors who do consulting. I have been amazed at Harvard how relatively few of our top-flight professors are on boards of directors. Another area is that of university heads. Anybody today who can run a major educational institution today is one hell of a capable administrator.

Secondly, I think major firm CPA's are a virtually untapped source, and in good part this is because of the CPA's themselves. They have had rules against it, but they are loosening up. Two things are happening: CPA firms are retiring their people earlier. At least one firm now retires its partners at age 55; most of the others no later than 60. Further, a number of CPA firms are willing to have their active partners sit on boards. They obviously cannot sit on boards of companies that they audit, but they are allowed to sit on other boards; and with the coming importance of the audit committee this is an extremely important role.

Economists are another possibility. I think business has by and large mistrusted economists. I think they are a good field to look for, particularly if you can find the right one. I am not saying I would recommend a left-wing economist to sit on any of your boards, but I think there are other economists that could.

I think another untapped source is potential CEO's. Many excellent CEO's of other companies will have been booked up by the time you try and fill a board spot, but in many companies it is pretty evident as to who is going to be the coming CEO. Why not reach for him?

Community leaders represent yet another source. John Johnson talked about this a little bit. This source is virtually untapped for major boards of directors. And these people have high visibility, and can be well checked out before they are brought on the board. I think this represents the best source for women and minority members.

Later, in this conference, I suspect, you will hear something about having labor on the board. And it is not inconceivable to me that some of you might be able to find the kind of labor leader who would make a very good board member. I don't think that I need to add that caution is extremely important in this area. But it is a coming thing.

Now, I'd like to talk about some hazards in selecting board members. I agree with Courtney Brown that we should keep away from tokenism. At best you will have a non-productive board member; at worst, you may be adding a very disruptive influence in board operations.

Secondly, watch out for conflicts of interest, whether apparent or real. Actually, independence is a state of mind, but the appearance of a conflict of interest must be avoided as well as the real thing. I don't know how many of you remember that in 1972 the FTC ordered John Meyer, the chairman of Mellon National Bank and Trust Company, to give up his directorship of either Alcoa or Armco on the ground that certain divisions of Alcoa were in competition with certain divisions of Armco.

Now, anyone who knows John Meyer is well aware that he felt no conflict of interest, but since it appeared he had one, something had to give. He resigned from the board of Armco in December, 1972. But what I worry far more about is the real conflict of interest that is not apparent. For example, one of the ablest outside directors I know is a partner in an investment banking concern. He is imaginative, practical, and experienced. His advice on matters discussed by the boards is thoughtful and helpful. Still, every time one of the companies of which he is a director needs additional equity money or long-term financing, his firm gets a major piece of the action, which frequently runs into hundreds of thousands of dollars.

Now, because he has intimate knowledge of and concern for the companies for which he is a director, one might reason that the investment banker could do a better financing job than anybody else. But it still worries me that this conflict of interest exists. Many CEO's I know would much prefer to have some competition for their investment banking business and they would wonder whether their friendly board member might be swayed in his decisions by the amount of his commissions. Some boards include two investment banker members employed by different firms. This arrangement might be best for a capital-intensive company.

It's been my experience that the price competition in commercial banking is so fierce and so open that a company's decision as to which should be the lead bank frequently depends on service and service frequently is better if the top man in a bank is on your board.

I found the same thing true by and large with corporate lawyers. In most of the situations I have seen the individual disassociates himself from active work on your account, but the very fact that he, a senior partner of the law firm, is sitting there, does mean that your service is great; and I have found that fees are shaved very frequently because one of the bosses is on your board.

I think another hazard is the individual with many directorships. Some people seem to acquire directorships the way some women acquire charms for their charm bracelets. While circumstances will vary from person to person, it is difficult to see how anyone could do an effective job if he or she has 10 or 12 directorships in addition to a full-time job.

Also, we ought to keep directors out of day-to-day operations. There's been considerable discussion of assigning a director the role of ombudsman. He could have a staff reporting to him and be responsible for overviewing a specific portion of the company's business. The major problem with this possibility is the tendency of the director, himself a successful businessman presumably, to get into operating decisions. And there is no better way to emasculate a CEO than that.

Finally, avoid retaining inside directors on boards when they are no longer full-time employees. For example, if a company has a normal retirement age of 65, inside directors should retire from the board at 65 as well. If a new CEO is brought in from outside the company, it may be desireable to have the retiring CEO stay on the board to furnish advice and counsel for a reasonable length of time, but certainly no more than a year.

Another problem is that of implied terms of office and the issue of tenure. I have more questions then answers here. This really shouldn't be a problem, but it frequently is, and for two reasons. First, a mistake can be made in your initial directorship selection; and secondly, a good director can lose interest or run out of steam. But getting a director off a board can be a problem ranging from hurt feelings to bad press.

The one-year term which most companies use is not real solution because it is expected that the directors will be re-elected. The three-year term, sometimes with a limitation of two terms in a row and then a year's absence is a step in the right direction, but I'd hate to lose a very good director for a year after he's had six years on the job. One board I know of pays a pension to directors at age 70 if they have had 10 years of service on the board, and I think this is a terrible precedent.

Speaking of retirement, different people react differently at different ages but I suggest a firm retirement age of 70 or 72 with the inside directors going off the board when they retire from the company.

Finally, who should be chairman? And here I differ with Courtney Brown. I can see an occasional case in which an outsider who can and will spend substantial time on company affairs might be the chairman of the board. Certainly it can't be an insider who reports to the CEO. I tend to favor the outsider who has breadth and maturity, but as I said a few minutes ago, never the former CEO.

I do feel the CEO as chairman can work very well if he has a strong board. He will talk individually and in groups with his most valuable directors and get playback in this way.

I'd like to wind up with the Lewis guidelines for selection of outside director candidates. The candidate should have:

1) outstanding business, administrative, or other valuable experience, proven ability, and significant accomplishments.

2) He should either hold a position of high responsibility or have recognized expertise in one or more areas.

3) He should have no present or visible potential for conflict of interest and should not be an officer or director of any a) major supplier to the company; b) major customer of the company; or c) competitor of the company.

4) He should contribute to the collective expertise of the board so that diversity of age, business, geographical location, area of endeavor, and viewpoint are represented in relation to the company's opportunities and responsibilities.

5) He should be able to show some connection with organizations which serve the community in civic, social, and charitable activities.

6) He should posses self-confidence and be at ease with individuals of distinguished attainment.

7) He should be articulate, but not garrulous, and command respect from peers.

8) He should possess maturity, but also display youthful initiative, enthusiasm, and a progressive attitude.

9) He should be independent of recent past or present directors.

10) He should be an existing or potential stockholder.

11) He should be enthusiastic about the prospect of serving and can devote the necessary time.

12) He should be neither chosen nor excluded solely because of race, color, or sex.

If I were to add a 13th, I think I would say if the man or woman could walk on water, it would be very helpful.

Question: This is for Mr. Brooker. What do you see in the role, if any, of the professional director?

Mr. Brooker: I believe there are occasions where you can well appoint a professional director. For example, I think Texas Instruments had Dr. Sykes as a professional director, an outstanding man in the field of research. It certainly fits in very well with the technology that they are engaged in. Ralph mentioned the thought of having a partner of an accounting firm, particularly on retirement. And a number of firms are appointing directors that have this background, and their principal responsibility is to chair the audit committee and make sure that you have an in-depth analysis of the audit.

Question: John, what are your views regarding the presence of a majority of so-called inside members, employee members, on a board? Do you have a ratio to recommend of inside versus outside directors?

Mr. Johnson: Yes. I think it is rather dangerous to have too many inside directors.

They would tend to advance their own individual policies. I would prefer something like one-third inside and two-thirds outside.

Question: Ralph, why is there not a data bank or pool showing a list of those interested in serving on a board? This would be a starting point in a search for new directors.

Mr. Lewis: I think that some of the executive recruiting firms are preparing that kind of thing as it is becoming, I wouldn't say it is common, but it is almost common to have an executive recruiting firm in many cases, and they are compiling data banks.

Question: Mr. Johnson, where does one go to meet top black people in business, education, or other suitable places?

Mr. Johnson: Well, that's a hard one. In the city of Chicago, I think we can do it in some of the private clubs now. We have the Economic Club in Chicago, the Executive Club, the Lion's Club, and so on, so that many of the clubs have black members. Now, other than that I would recommend such organizations as the Urban League, which is made up primarily of business and professional groups from various racial groups.

Question: Ralph, why not have a former CEO as chairman of the board?

Mr. Lewis: I am all for removing the dead hand of the past. When the new CEO is made CEO, he presumably has the responsibility, and if his former boss is sitting over his shoulder, this is no good.

Reinvigorating a Civilization

Clarence C. Walton

President, The Catholic University of America

Dr. Clarence C. Walton is the first lay president of The Catholic University of America. He previously taught at the University of Scranton and Duquesne University, and served as Dean of the School of Business Administration at Duquesne. He has also served as Associate Dean of the Graduate School of Business, and Dean of the School of General Studies at Columbia.

Dr. Walton has visiting professorships at many major universities, is the author of five books and co-author of four more, and has 40 or so articles in scholarly journals.

Because "change" is a household word today, it may be inferred that a word widely used, is well understood. The reverse may be nearer the truth. The successive collapses of various economic doctrines, artfully contrived to cope with changing business conditions, symbolizes the limits of our comprehension. Examples come readily to mind. Twenty years ago large numbers of business economists from the developed countries of the world consulted with leaders from less developed countries but their formula for "take-off" failed to bring results. A decade ago the RAND economist responsible for the planning-programming-budgeting system applied it to the Department of Defense and found that it did not work. The Bretton Woods Agreement, designed to stabilize international monetary and trading relationships, has been replaced by currency floats, competitive devaluations and special drawing rights, and these substitutions have meant the dismantling of this arrangement. Professor Kenneth Arrow, the Nobel Laureate, confessed that the coexistence of inflation and unemployment represents an uncomfortable fact in an intellectual riddle. The litany could be extended but it is sufficient for our purposes to suggest the existence of a riddle: the more we talk of change the less we seem to understand it!

Yet change is altering the heartland of western civilization and with these alterations come challenges to existing organizational structures: how they are manned, managed, monitored and maintained. While the challenges are formidable, they are not beyond the capacity of a nation which itself was conceived on the eve of an Industrial Revolution—an upheaval which transformed the lives, habits and structures of people more than any other single event in contemporary western history.

And because there is, at this Conference, a cadre of experts who have observed or analyzed boards, served on boards and resigned from boards, it may be inferred that from them will come *practical* suggestions to improve board performances. This inference suggests the wisdom of another approach—less practical and "how-to-do-it" and, more conceptual and historical. My thesis accepts the reality of change and the necessity for coping with it; it proceeds on the premise that wide perspectives are necessary and that such perspectives can be enhanced by consideration of three propositions:

(1) It is important to consider how business leadership emerges, flowers and declines; at this point a so-called "Pirenne Thesis" contains constructive lessons which merit restatement.

(2) The necessary task of reinvigorating American civilization requires not only a clear perception of its nature from those who manage it but imposes upon leadership new expository and advocacy roles.

(3) The current drift toward egalitarianism and participatory democracy introduces a significant new psychological element, namely, the idea that future leadership will be measured as much by life styles as by intellectual acumen.

An examination of each proposition leads to certain conclusions which have a cumulative impact on the way boards of the future are recruited, screened, organized, and staffed.

The Pirenne Thesis of Business Leadership

(A) The Thesis

The use of a name unknown to most American businessmen prompts two questions: Who is Pirenne? What is his argument? Henri Pirenne was a Belgian historian whose special expertise was the medieval period. Some sixty years ago, Pirenne wrote a fascinating essay, "Stages in the Social History of Capitalism" which appeared in the prestigious *American Historical Review.* Now forgotten, the article, in its time, generated considerable interest because this Belgian scholar rejected the notion of continuity in business leadership and argued that there is a distinct and separate class of capitalist for each major period. The class emerges from a lower social strata and, having nothing, is prepared to take risks to satisfy emerging needs. In the early stages of development, these entrepreneurs enjoy the widest possible freedom but their successes lead inexorably to two consequences: (1) they seek security and status in order to insulate themselves from competition, and (2) their power invites sharper regulation and more frequent intervention by public authorities. These "mature" business groups fail to make contact with changing economic conditions and are subsequently replaced by entrepreneurs who are more sensitive to new market opportunities. These new leaders of business then repeat the cycle in a Splenglerian rise-and-fall rhythm.

In applying the thesis to American business it may be argued that American history since the mid-nineteenth century traversed three distinct stages. First were the industrialists—the Vanderbilts and Carnegies, the Rockefellers and Edisons—who dominated American life in the late nineteenth century. The second phase, running from 1900 to 1930, witnessed the conquest by the "captains of finance" who, from their Wall Street offices, provided economic fuel for the nation's industrial engines. The third act of the drama began roughly in 1930 with the advent of the professional manager who became the indispensable and indisputable leader of American business. Berle and Means identified this evolution in 1932 and eventually hailed the manager as the lord "temporal" of the secular kingdom.

It must be quickly admitted that the American pattern does not precisely fit the Pirenne mold in the sense that the Belgian scholar concentrated on consumer needs; nevertheless the essential point in Pirenne (that a response to a particularly critical need would elicit a new class of business leader) appears to be vindicated by American business history.

Implicit in the Pirenne thesis are two very important lessons. There is a warning against excessive preoccupation with personal and professional status and security and there is, secondly, the challenge to leadership to identify and meet the neglected needs of society. This second "lesson" possesses intriguing possibilities, which are too infrequently exploited by major enterprises. To concretize this point let us suppose that members of a board are convened in a two or three day session and asked to write a list of questions which, in their judgment, constitute mankind's priorities. What would be the final result? Is the following decalogue representative or unrepresentative of board thinking?

(B) Critical Questions

(1) Why has productivity output per man in the period 1960–1973 been lower in the United States than in Japan, Germany, France, Canada, Italy, and the United Kingdom?

(2) What significance attaches to the fact that the rate of private investment in percent of gross national product was 18% for the United States (lowest among the seven nations mentioned above). What is the significance of the fact that Japan had a 33% rate for the same thirteen-year period?

(3) Are corporate profits excessive, adequate, inadequate? Recently, Treasury Secretary Simon declared that in 1973, after tax, profits of all corporations increased 27%, which on the surface appears to be a sparkling performance. However, a significant part of that increase represents gains in inventory evaluations attributable only to inflation. . . . In fact, undistributed corporate profits (after taking account of the inventory evaluation factor) increased only $3 billion last year—below the 1966 level.

(4) Is the primary crisis of America found in our energy shortage? Are new programs for conversion and the development of additional sources the nation's top priorities? This was suggested by Philip Abelson in the December 15, 1974 issue of *Science*.

(5) Is the major industrial malignancy found in worker dissatisfaction? According to the United States Department of Labor, the number of idle man-days due to work stoppages more than doubled during the last decade (from 20 million during the 1960's to an average of over 50 million during 1960–1970).

(6) Is the scandal of industrial America the very small proportion of income received by the poorest 20% in society—plus the further fact that this proportion has not responded to increases in the average standard of living?

(7) Will the future of American society depend on taming the strengthened bargaining power of organized labor and the enhanced economic power of large corporations?

(8) Has each corporation been so preoccupied with its own problems that it has failed to recognize, in Exxon's Mike Wright's words, "the interdependence of the total business community"? Will future boards be concerned with monitoring and reacting to matters affecting the *entire* business community?

(9) Is the greatest unmet need that of our urban centers? In March of 1971, when big city mayors gathered in Washington, their legislative action committee reported sadly that some cities, "like New Orleans, were taxing anything that moved and anything that stood still—and were still going broke." Should business leadership assist

in creating a new Urban Reserve Bank just as the nation once invented a Federal
Reserve System to meet the demands of a rapidly growing economy?

(10) Is the first task of business leadership found in the challenge of "crisis of
confidence"? Reporting in the *Saturday Review/World* of December 14, 1974, Norman
Cousins said: "We have the brainpower. We have the manpower. We have the technology. What we don't have . . . is confidence in ourselves, in our history, and in the
ultimate power of ideas."

Quite clearly, different minds with different perspectives and more informed
minds with broader views will generate different dialogues and different decalogues.
But the value of rethinking the Pirenne insight lies in its explicit invitation to identify
the critical needs of a changing society and, next, of moving aggressively to satisfy
such needs. Since the modern enterprise is a major engine for social and economic
change, it follows inescapably that those who direct it are inextricably involved in a
sequence of cause-and-effect actions which require constant attention. And this conclusion leads to our second proposition: the role of business leadership will increasingly involve both exposition and advocacy.

Exposition and Advocacy

The heavy burden of understanding and explaining the essential meaning of
society has always fallen on an elite. At one time it was the priest, at another it was
the scholar. Today it may be the Supreme Court justices, a small cadre of intellectuals,
or the media managers. Certainly since the days of the Warren court, judges have taken
an increasingly aggressive role in determining what is permissible and impermissible in
both corporate and personal morals. The views of what we are and how we came into
being are shaped by a limited number of journals and by an even smaller group of
great dailies such as the *Wall Street Journal,* the *Washington Post,* and the *New York
Times.*

Let us turn to the intellectuals for illustrative purposes. That they have been
hostile to business for a long time is generally known and with that knowledge comes
some small comfort. A sense of this persistent trend led the late Joseph Schumpeter
to conclude that the very successes of capitalism (and not its failure as Marx averred)
would bring its destruction if for no other reason than that the intellectual class would
be significantly enlarged and, as a consequence, its influence greatly expanded. History,
however, may turn out to be a poor guide if it leads to a comforting complacency
on the part of business.

What gives the intellectual a special importance today are three developments:
(1) massive enrollment increases, (2) politicalization and (3) anti-democratic stresses.
Since the war, enrollments have skyrocketed so that many universities have shifted
from a tradition of elitism to egalitarianism and, in the process, have accepted basic
changes in curriculum and in faculty recruitment. The December issue of The American
Academy of Arts and Sciences' *Daedalus,* reckoned with these massive increases and
concluded that with numbers has come a decline in quality. The second fact—and a
more ominous one—is the new politicalization which is striking major universities
in the western world. Berkeley has not fully recovered from the student riots of a
decade ago; neither has Columbia. Nevertheless, it may be suggested that, on balance,
American institutions of higher learning have regained a measure of equilibrium that
makes them the envy of their European counterparts. Oxford had a series of violent

student disturbances during 1973–4; West German universities are particularly vulnerable as faculty and student coalitions, dominated by Marxists, have won control in places like Marburg and Berlin. Accompanying these changes has been a rigidifying of doctrine and a growing determination to destroy the "bourgeois institutions." Since the key bourgeois institutions are private enterprise and parliamentary government, it is probable that both will face hard days ahead and both will require the firm adherence and support of its beneficiaries. Finally, it should be noted that added to the intellectuals' historic antibusiness sentiment is a growing cynicism toward democracy as well. This cynicism, particularly marked since Hawthorne's time, is obvious in the works of such towering creative geniuses as T. S. Eliot, Ezra Pound, and William Butler Yeats. Unalterably opposed to technology, science, commerce, and the levelling qualities of a democratic society, the influence of poets and writers may have shaped the thought processes of the young with greater subtlety than either Marx or Lenin.

If the foregoing assessment is true it follows that *a major challenge to board members in the future will be to understand, to explain, and to advocate—and to do all of these in arenas and from platforms which they have frequently found uncongenial.* If directors accept these assignments, certain caveats are in order. For one thing, heaping praise on our material achievements is not enough. While there is cause for pride in a country which reduced factory work hours from approximately 62 per week in 1870 to roughly 40 hours weekly in 1973 (while achieving simultaneously an 8½ times increase G.N.P. per capita) the stress must be made on a strong material base as prerequisite for a more fulfilling civilization and culture. It would be equally futile for business to mount a direct assault on the intellectual community. The real need is for dialogue, not confrontation, and business leadership, overwhelmed by its own concerns, has not been a ready or willing partner to such dialogue. Future boards will be structured to include those who have an understanding of, and appreciation for, American education. A director's involvement in matters of concern to higher education is neither to control nor to be controlled but rather to understand and to be understood. This interest will likely extend to other powerful "influence" organizations in our society: churches, mass media, labor unions, large voluntary organizations, and consumer movement groups. It is doubtful that American society can continue to perpetuate the "good-guy and bad-guy" syndrome and business leadership should be among the first seeking to dismantle this destructive kind of adversary relationship.

This position should be differentiated from advocacy. The distinctions will be hard to maintain in practice but certainly directors who go to Washington to advance a piece of legislation or to inhibit the progress of another are engaged in advocacy roles. And the director should come, not as a registered lobbyist seeking only special attention for a single enterprise, but rather as one concerned with the survival and success of the free-enterprise system. Congressmen, regulators and executives need to demonstrate a common willingness to listen and to talk back—and to do both under the watchful eye of an affected public who recognizes that honest men may differ on means to achieve common goals.

Above all, advocacy requires a sense of enthusiasm that what one is doing is important and worth the investment. Business leadership consists not simply of jobs but of challenges which accept the premise that free men are led, never driven. Like creativity in any endeavor, there will be high points and low points but the sense of excitement and fulfillment—as Alfred North Whitehead has so eloquently reminded us—must be kept alive. And this sense requires a measure of learning and sophistication.

Is this summons too quixotic and too impracticable to be of serious concern to business leadership? Having advanced the proposition, it is obvious that I think not. Each month produces dramatic examples of insights into the importance of a free society which go unnoted to become lost opportunities for public instruction. One thinks, for example, of what must—by any account—be ranked as a major television program in recent history when the speaker was heard to say the following:

> The only way out of our unhappy situation is to achieve a complete renaissance of the market, the instrument best fitted to gauge the success or failure of enterprises. . . . After twenty years of taking orders, management teams will have to accustom themselves to the hitherto unknown feeling that, without orders, advice, or approval from the top, they will be obliged to make full use of their own ideas. Indeed, with the market recording every failure, every lag behind world standards, with the precision of a boomerang, it will be forced to do so.

These words were uttered by Dr. Ota Sik, then deputy premier of Czechoslovakia, to all the citizens of that unhappy land. If American viewers could have shared vicariously in the Czechoslovakian experience—including the breaches of Czech frontiers by Soviet tanks—powerful lessons of history might have been shared with American audiences.

One recalls, too, the reactions of Daniel Moynihan as reported in the *Washington Post* of December 15, 1974 to his experiences as Ambassador to India. Comparing India's steel industry to Japan's, Mr. Moynihan observed:

> When India won its independence from Britain in 1947, it was producing 1.2 million tons of steel a year. That was just after World War II and Japan was producing 800,000 tons. Twenty-five years later, India's output had risen to 6.8 million tons while Japan's had surged to 106.8 million tons. The Japanese achieved this spectacular gain despite having to import iron ore and coal to fire their furnaces, while India had mammoth deposits of both.

Moynihan's conclusion is pertinent: *societies get the kind of economies they desire.* There may be no better single-sentence statement of the issue than this! Objective comparative studies of different economies constitute one of the most singular omissions of the business community's effort to explain or to advocate. This, coupled to too much negativism on important bits of social legislation, are legacies that must be modified for wider understanding if the American enterprise system is to be achieved. In all of this the Board will necessarily play the crucial role.

A Matter of Style

It has been suggested that the drift toward egalitarianism in a participatory democracy is likely to continue and that its continuance has implications for business leadership. Because the principle of parsimony becomes a necessity, specificity is given to this proposition by juxtaposing only two illustrative observations. The first is from an article in the *Harvard Business Review* (November–December, 1973) where this advice is given to "the ambitious executive":

Give outward evidence of status, power, and material success. Most people measure a leader by the degree of pomp and circumstance with which he surrounds himself. (This is why the king lives in a palace and the Pope in the Vatican). Too much modesty and democracy in his way of life may easily be mistaken for a lack of power and influence. For example, most subordinates take vicarious pride in being able to say, "That's my boss who lives in the mansion on the hill and drives a Rolls-Royce".

Yet a hundred years ago, Alexis de Tocqueville, one of the most perceptive observers of American ways and coiner of the famous concept of "individualism" to describe the American social system, observed that any display of wealth infuriated the American people. It was in this tradition that Justice Holmes once observed that a general starts to lose his command when he begins to worry over the size of his tent. Business leadership will find in de Tocqueville and Holmes better mentors.

The business elite constitute no royalty exercising imperial powers; neither are they secular priesthood. But there is more to the new egalitarianism than merely enjoinders for personal behavior. The widening net of democratic involvement challenges the conventional wisdom. This was enunciated in 1950 by Winthrop Aldridge, Chairman of the Chase Manhattan Bank, when he said that, "the management of this institution is in the hands of the directors. . . . The stockholders have no right to intervene!" The enterprise of the future will admit that the Aldridge aphorism is an anachronism. The corporations' public is more than the board or management, more than the stockholders and customers, more than suppliers and government. Given the interdependence of the society a good board will include members who themselves have access to all major currents in a highly fluid society: education and labor, philanthropy and church, government and media.

Conclusions

The thrust of my analysis has been toward those newly pressing activities which command a board member's interest and which go beyond the single enterprise. In no way does this suggest any dilution of a director's responsibility to the enterprise he has been asked to serve. Rather it means that, like charity, his duty begins at home—but does not end there. In this context the following generalizations may be advanced.

1. Recalling Pirenne, it should be recognized that the agenda of every major enterprise is interlocked with the agenda of the nation and of the world. Since the Full Employment Act of 1946, government has been heavily involved in economic decision-making. Society has generated rising expectations. Rising expectations mean new demands. Business will either respond to these new demands or forfeit initiative and responsibility to public authorities. The future Director will know the workings of business *and* of government.

2. If, as Schumpeter argues, the intellectual class will become increasingly anti-business, it is important that corporations become concerned with education. Involvement by certain Board members in the work of those other organizations which significantly influence America will become important. While the Director may remain a "generalist" he will be a quite sophisticated one.

3. As the enterprise becomes increasingly complex and operates in a complex milieu, management will be hard put to keep the store in order. Mounting demands on the chief executive lend credence to the thesis advanced by Courtney Brown for division of labor between the chief executive and the board chairman.

4. Boards will meet more frequently and for longer periods in order to monitor management performance and to assess the business climate.

5. Interlocking directorships will become less common because demands on a director's performance will escalate.

6. Advanced seminars for directors will become as commonplace as the present executive training programs for managers.

7. Experiments in rotation of key personnel will be undertaken. For example, enterprises may see the appointment of "paired peers" which permit one individual of the pair to serve as president for a given tenure while the other serves as board chairman—and both with knowledge that the roles are planned to be reversed.

8. The anonymity of board members will be attenuated as directors take public positions on controversial issues.

9. Conflict-of-interest codes will become more important and may well become part of the external audit.

10. The rather common practice of trying to present a united business front on controversial issues will end. For good reasons, board members of different companies may take strongly different views in public, relying on the Jeffersonian maxim that the market place of ideas is the best guarantee for a free and effective society.

Choosing a board will be more deliberate. Serving on a board will be more exhilarating. Performing well will be more difficult. Restricting one's commitments to a few boards will be more necessary.

International Investment:
Constraints and Incentives

William J. Casey

The Export–Import Bank of the U.S.

William J. Casey is President and Chairman of the Export-Import Bank of the United States. Previously he served as Chairman of the Securities and Exchange Commission, and Under Secretary of State for Economic Affairs. While Under Secretary of State, he served concurrently as Alternate Governor of the World Bank, the Inter-American Development Bank, and the Asian Development Bank. He is now a Member of the Commission on the Organization of the Government for the Conduct of Foreign Policy and has previously served on the General Advisory Committee on Arms Control and the Presidential Task Force on International Development.

Before his appointment as Chairman of the Securities and Exchange Commission, Mr. Casey was Chairman of the Board of Editors, Institute for Business Planning (1953–71), and a partner in the New York City law firm of Hall, Casey, Dickler and Howley (1957–71).

It is a pleasure to take part in this corporate director's conference to talk to you about international investment and the constraints and incentives which currently function on the international investment scene. Certainly, it is no discovery to this audience that international investment is currently and has been shaping the future course of history as profoundly as wars have done in the past. Through extension of sound credits for the development of human and natural resources, wealth has been created, essential materials are more widely distributed, and modern progress is reaching out to remote corners of the earth.

I am talking about what is being done with profit seeking investments, not about concessionary or development type loans. Aid has its place, but venture investments count most. It takes a profit incentive to induce capital to take risks, just as it does to bring out human effort.

The great bulk of foreign investing is still done by the United States. Our total assets abroad at the end of last year amounted to amost a quarter of a trillion dollars, with direct investments, mostly by our multinational corporations, accounting for more than half. Earnings from those investments are very important toward a balance of international payments on which the strength of the dollar and indeed the price level in this country depends.

In the first six months of 1974 our income from direct investment abroad was over $9 billion. By contrast, foreign investments here earned $2.8 billion. Their investments here at the end of 1973 amounted to about $17 billion and their earnings total was less than one-third of our earnings abroad.

Now, there are some technical factors involved in this tripling of foreign earnings in our country in six months, but there is a sharp trend in that direction that represents an emerging pattern that will require adjustment in many American attitudes. For example, Japanese investment in the steel mill in Auburn, New York, or a soy sauce plant in Wisconsin or a TV assembly plant on the west coast or real estate ventures in many places, and hopefully Arab oil investments in many types of enterprises here must be welcomed as additions to our job-producing economy and not frowned on as competitive encroachments. The climate we provide for foreign investments here can be expected to influence the reception of our investments abroad, and these foreign investments abroad will earn enough to offset more than half of the staggering costs of our mineral fuels imports this year.

When measuring our earnings on direct investments abroad, we should always note that our fee and royalty payments for foreign uses of our advanced technology are running ten to one in our favor. We earned $2 billion abroad in fees and royalties in the first half of 1974, while foreigners earned $200 million.

Now, it is easy to talk here among ourselves about the mutual benefits of foreign investment. But the fact is that the operation of our multinational corporations, the main form of our investments, is widely misjudged both at home and abroad. Fears that our multinational corporations are exporting American jobs are much more loudly expressed than is our industries' explanation that their purpose in branching out abroad is to gain competitive advantage in having production facilities located within or closer to foreign markets or to sources of raw materials. Relatively rare instances of where our multinational corporations send back foreign made goods to the United States are allowed to blur the fact that 90 percent of what they produce abroad stays abroad; that much of this is business they would lose to foreign competitors if they had to depend on production facilities at home, and that all major companies report substantial increases in domestic employment resulting from their overseas operation. We still hear the chorus that this results in the export of jobs, and not any appraisal or offsetting of the increase in jobs abroad or the increase in markets or the maintenance of markets that this process achieves. A company is naturally going to supply its overseas affiliate from home production whenever there is an advantage in doing so.

Now, suffering from this same lack of understanding are the contributions to U.S. domestic employment made by foreign investments here. Not only does this foreign investment provide us with economic growth, it relieves pressure on domestic capital markets, and that is becoming terribly important today. For its part, the business community is more likely to gain the American worker's understanding of the value of foreign investment if it takes cognizance of the dislocation in employment caused by these new trade shifts. The present trend is toward interdependence, with each nation relying on each other's skills and resources, each one concentrating on what it can fulfill best and fulfilling the rest of its needs by buying from others what they are better suited to produce. That's the way it is always started.

Now, with this international division of labor, the United States with its high technology is turning more from producing goods to providing services, using its engineering, financial, and managerial skills. And that is what has to happen when two out of three Americans now earn their living by performing services; only one-third of our labor force is engaged in the production of goods. This shift began in recent years as a result of our rising technology and productivity in meeting domestic demand,

and has now been accelerated by worldwide reliance on our know-how and technology. It is a challenge to our businessmen, however, and the manner in which they respond by helping retrain and relocate production workers displaced by these changing employment patterns, is what will determine how much future resistance we encounter to overseas expansion by U.S. business.

Meanwhile, foreign attitudes toward our overseas investments are mixed. Generally, American capital and enterprise are welcomed abroad up to a point. It is well understood that U.S. investments bring jobs, tax revenue, and in some cases badly needed export earnings. Host countries like to see technology along with our financing, organizing, production, and marketing abilities applied to the development of their own resources and their own country. And some less developed countries encourage certain forms of investment with grants, low interest loans, tax advantages and tax incentives. These inducements are usually offered for special purposes, mostly for regional development. While they may not produce the best possible results for investor dollars, since they draw investments away from more efficient uses to which the money might otherwise be put, nevertheless, their practice is very much like that followed by many U.S. communities as they go out and seek new industry to develop their own employment and economies.

So we have this tug of war for the investment dollar among countries, this conflict of attitudes. And there is uneasiness in many countries over the influence foreign corporations may be able to exert over the domestic economy and the domestic labor force. In these countries where there are labor surpluses, requirements for employment of host country personnel are the general rule and any sizeable use of expatriate personnel tends to be suspect. In the European community, where until recently there have been labor shortages, there are fears that changes in the production patterns in the multinational corporations operating across member borders may cause labor force disruptions.

Less developed countries are pushing for worker participation in management decisions. This idea has gained the advocacy of the officially designated "Group of Eminent Persons," a 21-man panel appointed by the United Nations Economic and Social Council. Their eminences have filed a report urging not only increased worker authority over MNC management operations, but also proposing that in disagreements between a multinational corporation and a host country, international arbitration or persuasion from the home country be rejected, thus stripping the company of any outside recourse. Among the eminent persons' other recommendations which they would like to see enforced by treaty law is one revising the patent system to provide technology to less developed countries at lower costs.

Failure to adapt to host country industrial practices causes some complaints, perhaps some valid ones, although in extreme cases indigenous producers can be found operating mostly by intuition, paternalism, and nepotism, with the owners' relatives holding most key jobs and with sales effort confined largely to personal relationships—and customer service getting indifferent attention at best. When it is a matter of transferring U.S. management knowhow to an enterprise that will be operated by indigenous personnel trained under a system like that, the process becomes an exercise in adaptation of computerized efficiencies to *la dolce vita.* Think of the problem an American corporation would have in granting local autonomy to an overseas affiliate operating in that style.

To illustrate the point, the story is told of an American businessman who visited a government office out in the boondocks on a weekday afternoon. He found no one in the plant but the janitor. He looked around and said, "It seems they don't work here in the afternoons." And the janitor said, "Oh, it is the mornings they don't work. In the afternoons they don't come."

We see requirements also for local equity participation in an enterprise directed from abroad, or for exporting fixed percentages of production, or for use of host country commodities. Very often the developers in these countries are required to provide educational, job training, and health facilities in the area of operation. And U.S. developers do this anyway for industrial and community relations purposes, but it is sometimes a burden that is required in rather substantial portions.

Now, even a developed country like Canada can reserve the right to limit the size of the foreign investments or may require that R & D facilities be set up in the host country. Indonesia, for example, requires developers of its raw materials to process them or refine them before shipment from that country. This is a reservation that at least one country, Japan, looks on with favor, as it serves the Japanese purpose of locating more of such projects abroad for environmental reasons at home. And we see the Japanese in their five-year plan seeking to export labor intensive, energy intensive, and polluting industries. And we see the Germans, before the recent recession set in, becoming concerned that they had reached the limits of their ability to expand their industry by bringing workers in from Turkey, Yugoslavia, and Portugal, plus other places in southern Europe—a limit to the amount of social disruption that process created and they could stand. And six months ago they shifted their policy, attempting to move the plants out to where the workers are instead of the workers to where the plants are. So we do have some substantial forces operating to move industry out to less developed areas for reasons of a social rather than financial or economic character.

There are other areas of controversy that are getting attention from the OECD and other international bodies. The charge is heard widely, for example, that multinational corporations manage to avoid their fair share of taxes, in some cases, by transferring pricing; in other words, setting prices arbitrarily in transactions between parent and overseas affiliates or between affiliates and different countries, so as to make the profits show up in the country where the taxes are lowest. There are complaints about the disruptive effect of movement of short-term capital by multinational corporations, and controversies over licensing practices and transfers of technology.

OECD, the group of 24 industrialized countries, with which the U.S. cooperates closely and which is probably a better forum for thrashing out these problems than the United Nations, is now working on the development of a code of conduct among multinational enterprises, and we can expect gradual progress to be made in these areas because of the increasing imperatives for cooperation in world economic development.

Unfortunately, however, advances in mutual understanding and in the working out of conflicts of economic purpose and procedural disagreements will still leave the investment climate heavily influenced by a tightening grip on available investment capital. The picture is one of steeply rising demand on the one hand and a rapid sequestration of capital by oil producing countries on the other; in short, capital formation. It is today occurring in one small part of the world. And new opportunities abound for profitable investment in massive developments of future sources of food, energy, and minerals, and in other highly viable types of projects over much of the world.

Heavy inputs of equity and loan capital also are needed by businesses trying to employ better technology and equipment and keep growing in the face of highly inflated costs.

It has come to the point, speaking from current experiences at the Export-Import Bank, where all kinds of ingenious arrangements and many months of negotiating are necessary in putting together a financing package for a high priority commercial overseas project, such as the nuclear power plant or a mining venture costing hundreds of millions of dollars. Public and private money from both at home and abroad, including commercial bank syndications, Eurodollar borrowings, and government guaranteed participations have to be combined in a single project. And some projects which would be feasible in times of higher liquidity and single digit interest rates now have to be deferred.

A big part of the remedy for this must involve getting the petrodollars into overseas investing. Failure to get this money back into productive use is already causing trouble in the oil producing countries themselves. Some of the consequences of the present conditions are amazing. For example, in the first nine months of 1974 we had a deficit of $2.3 billion in merchandise trade. That was approximately the same amount of our deficit with each of two individual oil producing countries, Venezuela and Nigeria. In short, we ran a deficit with Venezuela and Nigeria separately at the same level as our deficit with the rest of the world. Our deficit with each of those countries was twice as much as it was with Japan. Our deficit for these two countries combined was larger than our favorable balance with western Europe.

And we see from press reports that this situation is inflicting domestic damage. Petrodollar food has thrown Venezuela into a state of inflation emergency. The president there has been granted authority to raise wages 25 percent, impose luxury taxes, cancel debts of farmers, prepare plans for expansion of industry, agriculture, and public works, speed up amortization of the country's foreign debt, and put half the country's oil revenues into United States Treasury paper, and loans to other Latin American countries.

So we see frantic efforts to put this accumulation of money into some kind of useful circulation while opportunities for sound investment in viable projects around the world go begging. I went to three countries in the Middle East last month to talk about the possibilities of attracting petrodollar financing in which our technology and equipment would be used to develop new sources of scarce materials. There was interest in the general idea. Certainly these countries are setting up new institutions to invest abroad, both for developing purposes and to get investments for themselves; and the order of priority for these investments would be home country projects first, then projects of the Arab and Moslem world, then agricultural type projects in nearby African countries, and this is a beginning. I think ultimately they will make some of their funds available for participation in natural resource development projects, particularly on a worldwide basis.

And at the Bank we also believe that further sources of export project financing can be found in the private sector at home. Pension funds, certain forms of trusts, and thrift institutions might benefit from long-term project investments fully backed by Export-Import Bank guarantees. We have found some support in the private sector for this idea and we think we can diversify the participation in export financing beyond the commercial banks over to the institutional investors in one form or another.

Now, to round out the list of constraints to international investments, there is the issue of doing business with the Communist countries in which common prudence as well as regulations on both sides of the transaction come into play. Opportunities will consist mostly of specific U.S. export transactions with state financing. No Communist country, except Yugoslavia, authorizes direct western investment. Also Romania. Those two countries allow up to 49 percent equity and have devices which enable westerners to participate in, and repatriate, profits. Otherwise, business deals with the bloc countries are mostly of the joint venture type, involving special production or marketing or banking arrangements whereby you invest in the project, you put the project together, and you get paid back, for the most part, from a portion of the production, or proportion of the production proceeds, when it is sold abroad.

Other financing to the Soviet Union and other Communist countries is supervised directly by the Administration and Congress. To the extent permitted, bankers tend to grant credit to the Soviets on much the same basis as anyone else on the theory that virtually anything they buy from the U.S. they can get elsewhere on credit supported by the governments of the supplying countries. Also that restrictions on purchases from us will not impair the expansion of their economies or the carrying out of their development projects, but will simply mean that our suppliers would lose the business and the business would go somewhere else and the financing will be forthcoming from other countries.

Today I guess western European countries and Japan put together have loaned about five times as much to the Soviet Union as the United States has. It might be said in summary of restraints on overseas investments that they represent pillars of ideology, nationalism, and economic self-interest that are bending but not breaking under pressures for cooperation for mutual benefit. The prevailing world influence is interdependence. Americans are, after all, doing business anywhere in the world they choose now. Their sales to the People's Republic of China will amount to almost $1 billion this year.

The main incentive for overseas investment has already been touched upon: profit opportunities, especially for funds that can be made available for long-term project financing and provide new sources of scarce and vital materials. This is the economic equation which has to come into play in the world. We have the equipment, the technology, managerial skills. Mostly the lesser developed countries have the fibers, the land, the natural resources, and, increasingly, oil producing countries have the capital. And the whole international investment scene has to blend together and put together our equipment and technology and managerial skills with the natural resources around the world and with the capital that is accumulating within the oil producing countries.

Competition for sources of supply is becoming as basic a force in trade as competition for markets. One reason is a tendency among supplier countries to limit the export of essential materials to meet their own essential needs. Canada, for example, is cutting back on oil exports to the United States. Or it may be a matter of holding down export earnings to reduce domestic inflation, to keep processing jobs at home or to take advantage of higher prices. This spurs the search for new supply sources with investment profitability following a rising curve of need for materials in short supply.

And a further incentive for U.S. investments in export credits is our country's heavy reliance on sales of high technology goods and services. Our exports of long-range commercial jet aircraft, nuclear power plants, agribusiness projects, mineral projects, engineering and construction services, with all their follow-on business for America's equipment suppliers, are the source of much of the world's progress and of our own position in world trade.

These sales frequently derive from big ticket transactions which call for financing in larger amounts and on longer terms than are readily available from commercial banks. They depend on investments that go beyond the usual channels. You must remember, too, that incentives work for others as well as us. If we want petrodollar investments in this country to relieve the pressure on domestic capital, we should think about making investment opportunities here more attractive.

The Treasury eliminated direct controls on foreign investments and the interest equalization tax. The next logical step would be to eliminate withholding taxes on interest and dividends that go out of the U.S. to foreign holders of U.S. securities.

Now, the case for and against international investment has been prejudged in these remarks. The verdict clearly favors more investments. Many old trade barriers, including those of iron and bamboo, are coming down in recognition of the mutual benefits to be gained by exchanging resources. Part of the job is to reduce the remaining ones to a bare minimum. New constraints are being churned up in the struggles against inflation, rigged oil prices, mounting trade deficits, and shortages of basic materials. The rest of the job is to discourage new barriers wherever possible.

And despite all obstacles, despite the pressures to maintain current accounts and to avoid currency devaluations and trade restrictions, to maintain the dollars necessary to pay for the oil the countries need around the world, I am confident that progress can be made in both directions. We had a very encouraging development over the weekend in the final enactment of the trade bill after about 14 months or 16 months of struggle, and this is an opportunity that I hope we will be able to capitalize on to resist pressures for trade restrictions, to open up trade around the world, and to open up the flow of foreign investment around the world.

And to accomplish that we are going to have to resist the effort to restrict investments within the United States and we are going to have to resist the effort to keep our capital home and to insist on it being used wherever it can be used most effectively in the world. Thank you.

Question: Mr. Casey, you didn't comment at all on this petrodollar flow into the U.S., the threat, or are there any constraints being considered with respect to Middle Eastern investments in the U.S.?

Mr. Casey: Well, Mr. Mueller, there is no constraint being considered by the Administration. I think a majority of the Congress believes it would be unwise to impose any constraints in the sense of prohibitions. I believe there will be some legislation which will provide for a closer monitoring of foreign investments so we know what is flowing in here and we do now have constraints existing, prohibitions against foreign investments beyond certain points in sensitive industries, defense industries, banks, television stations, newspapers, and so on.

And it is my view this is all that we should have and I think that is the Administration's view. I think Congress will sustain that position.

Question: What is the cost of technology royalty? Why is the cost of technology a problem since it amounts to only one percent approximately of the total capital investment in licensed plants? Why is it a problem, the cost of technology?

Mr. Casey: Well, I don't think it is a problem. I think there are some countries who don't like to pay because it seems like an intangible. They don't seem to understand they are getting something for it. My own view is just the other way, what I worry about with respect to technology is whether we are selling it too cheap, whether we are selling too many turnkey deals in which the technology goes abroad and we shortcut a long-term trade thereby.

I think the government can't monitor that, it has to depend upon the self-interests of the owners of the technology to get whatever they can for it. But from the standpoint of our government policy, our only complaint is we don't get enough for the technology. Other countries think it is an intangible. Mexicans have a law which I think prohibits the approval of any payment for technology.

Question: What loans are available to U.S. institutions or firms? Are there guarantees by the Export-Import Bank? What eventually are these dollars used for?

Mr. Casey: Well, that gives me an opportunity to make a 45 minute speech about the Export-Import Bank. Let me just say that we probably make $6 or $8 billion worth of commitments a year in loans or guarantees for the purpose of enabling buyers of U.S. technology and equipment to buy and pay for the U.S. exports, and they are required to pay us back over whatever the appropriate period of time is. Over about 30 years we have collected everything, we have only charged off 2 cents out of every $100 we have loaned, and this money goes to the U.S. manufacturer or exporter, it never leaves the country, and he ships the products abroad and we are obligated to the buyer to pay us back.

Putting the Knowledge and Know-How of Outside Directors to Work

PART ONE

Willard F. Rockwell, Jr.

Rockwell International Corp.

Willard F. Rockwell, Jr. is Chairman of the Board of Rockwell International Corporation, and a Director of: Allegheny Ludlum Industries, El Paso Natural Gas Co., Kearney & Trecker Corp., Lone Star Industries, Inc., Mellon National Corp., Mellon Bank, N.A., Pittsburgh Testing Laboratory, and Merex, S.A., Buenos Aires, Argentina. In addition, he is an Advisory Director of El Paso Products Co., Odessa, Texas.

Mr. Rockwell is a Trustee of the United States Council of the International Chamber of Commerce, a Director of the U.S.–U.S.S.R. Trade and Economic Council, a member of the Advisory Council on International Commerce for the Commonwealth of Pennsylvania, and a member of the Board of Governors of the Pennsylvania Manufacturers' Association.

There are many viewpoints about the functions, responsibilities, and even the worth of boards of directors. For my part I am a working management type involved on a frequent basis with a pretty competent board of directors.

In top management we have to live with the world of boards of directors and not *part* of the world—the outside director world or the inside director world, or the director/committee world—but the entire board as a unit. And the chairman with his president, or perhaps sometimes his chief executive officer, may participate in the direction of perhaps a multi-billion dollar corporation and have a responsibility to scores of thousands of shareowners and perhaps 100,000 to 200,000 employees. At the same time he or she may participate in board decisions that could have a direct or indirect impact on the welfare of a city, a state, or even the nation.

So viewed from that seat of responsibility rather than through the keys of a typewriter, a board of directors takes on a different aspect from that of a rhetorical essay in a business magazine or a classroom lecture in an economics school. And that remark isn't directed at the academicians present. In the eyes of the chairman, the board of directors are not laboratory specimens, but real people with a crucial role in our free enterprise system.

In a *New York Times* article I read recently, it said, "Many managements are getting a little frantic in their hunt for untraditional outside directors." Well, I agree about that frantic atmosphere and I think it is quite unnecessary. It seems to me that the stirring around we see today as some companies seek the perfect board is almost humorous. Recently I received a letter from a head hunter who specializes in finding women directors. I think in the past few years we have seen too much of this striving for what is termed a balanced board, a quota system, you might say; a representation on the board of major corporations of minorities, women, and new college grads, and even consumer representatives.

Those people deserve representation, of course, but they deserve a place on the board only if they have something to contribute, and that something should fall in the realm of absolute dedication, absolute integrity, and a broad experience in economic, political, and social activities. To my mind to bring a black person, woman or young person on the board should not be attributed to his blackness, her femininity, or his or her youth, or his or her concern for the social well-being of our nation.

Louis Cabot, chairman of the board of Cabot Corporation, stated very well when he said, "In both fact and spirit, minority representatives must fully recognize that their first responsibility is the welfare of the corporation and its role in the total society. At the same time, minority representatives must be given assurance that their voice is heard within the corporate team."

The board of directors is not a showcase. It is a working body with a serious purpose and a serious legal responsibility. That serious business has been a fact of life for 40 years, ever since the Securities and Exchange Act of 1934. Moral intensity is not a substitute for competence.

And certainly being on a board isn't like going to the movies. A board member doesn't get a free seat in the gallery to watch the show. It is not a risk-free operation. The board member is a part of the action.

Also he can't pick and choose as to whom he is serving when he sits on the board. He gets the whole package, and the actions can affect the welfare of the share-owners, the welfare of the employees. In major corporations where there are broad consequences, the director's action can affect entire communities. It is even conceivable that his actions could affect to some degree similarly the welfare of the nation. He cannot put on a consumer's hat today and say, "I am a consumer director," and another hat tomorrow and say, "I am an inside director," and another hat the third day and say, "I am a minority representative director." If you are a director, you pick up every hat and you pick it up at every meeting.

Most men sitting at the board tables throughout the country know the need for balance and pursue it without any directives. And I think with me they share the conviction that the label of outsider or insider or lawyer or investment banker doesn't mean nearly as much as what quality of person is involved, his dedication, absolute integrity, and wealth of experience in national, international, economic, political, and social matters. I think these are the qualities sought by a chief executive officer when looking for new members to serve on a board of directors.

I have served as president, chief executive officer, chairman of the board, and director of a few American companies for some 35 years, and I am always conscious of the need for board members of wide experience in the legal and financial world to help guide me in carrying out my executive responsibility. In addition, it doesn't take a great deal of experience to recognize the advantages of having solid inside management sitting on the board. Who can better interpret the immediate needs, immediate strengths, and the weaknesses of a corporation than the men who have those concerns with them 24 hours a day?

Of course, there have been changes in the composition of boards during the years that I have been a board watcher. There has been more and more of a tilt toward outside directors in the percentage makeup. Seven years ago our board had 25 members, 11 inside and 14 outside. That was about a 45–55 percentage breakdown. And today we have five inside directors and 13 outside directors, about 30–70 percentagewise, in favor of the outside. That percentage, of course, might vary according to your personal definitions just what you consider an outsider.

As far as Rockwell International is concerned, the 70 percent participation by outsiders on our board is a sign of our search for invaluable experience as the company moves into more and more diversified fields. If I can give you an example, last year we made an important move in the consumer area, and almost overnight with the acquisition of the Admiral Corporation, some 11 percent of our total of $4.4 billion in sales was in the consumer market.

When we looked for a new member of the board after the Admiral acquisition, we used the standards we apply to all prospective board members without exception: dedication, absolute integrity, and wealth of experience. In this case our emphasis was on experience in consumer operations. It was our good fortune to get Ed Donnell, president of Marcor, to accept a position on our board. Almost immediately we could utilize with Ed one of the criteria for outside directors, that they act as advisors in areas where their general specialized background and experience can be applied to a specific problem of the company.

We needed a consultant who was an expert in marketing and consumer products, and of all people at Montgomery Ward, Ed Donnell should know the expert in that field. So we asked Ed for some candidates and he told us and we got a good man.

Several years ago we were debating some long-term financing for the corporation and in the opinion of the majority of the board the time was right to do it. But we had four banking members on the board at that time, and they said while we should increase our long-term debt, they advised us to hold off, our timing was bad. We accepted their judgment, delayed the financing for three months, and the result was a million-dollar-a-year savings for the corporation when we were able to get better interest rates.

I don't think there's ever been a major financial move made at Rockwell since 1967 that we haven't had our treasurer's staff sit down with our banking board members, the chairman, and the president, and discuss the matter of how we should do it, and the timing of it with them.

Another example. For years the oil companies sounded the alarm about the coming energy shortage, and very few people listened to that, as many of you know, until last year when the Arabs spoke the loudest by closing the pipeline. Before that happened, Fred Hartley, chief executive officer of the Union Oil Company and one of our directors, gave us the warning there would be an energy problem. We have been reading those warnings from the press, but sitting there in the board room listening to a man who knew what he was talking about made a difference.

As a result of his cautionary words, we started strenuous research on our energy needs as early as 1972. A committee of employees was given top priority to survey our operating needs for coal, oil, and natural gas. They determined the quantities we were using, what our resources were, what our reserves were, what steps we were taking to conserve those resources. When the full impact of the energy crisis came last year we were hurt, of course, but the impact was softened considerably because of the actions we had taken, which included even the purchase of some gas wells in response to the advice of a very valuable board member.

Last May I was in the Soviet Union exploring some contract possibilities in power conversion. This, of course, is a highly technical area, and I needed all the help I could get in discussing possibilities with different trade ministries in Moscow in evaluating the Soviet developments. I took along our own expert from our Operating Division, but I also asked Bill Crawford, one of our advisory directors and one of the country's leading authorities on power conversion, to join the group. I needed his detached, disinterested observations before we committed ourselves to something substantial one way or another.

These are examples of the close-in, immediate use we make of our outside directors. I agree completely with Dean Courtney Brown when he says the board of directors is the appropriate unit for the establishment of broad policies and procedures and for reviewing performance. In fact, I quoted him rather extensively in setting new objectives for our board just last November.

Outside directors bring a broad perspective to discussions of long-range policies and strategic plans. They are sounding boards for problems, a tremendous asset to the corporation. Because in management we need an impartial assessment of our activities, I know that we do a better job because the outside members sitting there in review are a very knowledgeable group of peers.

I won't dwell on salary, stock option, and incentive compensation committees that are set up on the boards. These are more or less standard throughout the corporate world and it makes sense that outside directors should set policy in these specific areas. We even ask them to respond to the stockholders about such problems in the stockholders' meeting.

The board's audit committee is assuming greater importance in these uncertain economic times. Most major company's boards of directors have had audit committees, but, very frankly, they haven't been too effective. They haven't always acted as they should in interfacing between management and the public auditing firms. In a few cases they have been neglected and some of that neglect, unfortunately, has tarnished the corporate image. In extreme cases, the neglect has had the effect of putting the entire corporate system on trial. That is why I think we should put greater emphasis on, and give more responsibility to, the audit committee.

It should be made a more effective committee and that, of course, opens up a wide range of discussion. We are discussing some of it right now in our company. Should we give the board audit committee a staff to identify issues, make investigations, do analyses, and predict trends? The idea is interesting, but I am personally appalled at the thought of creating another empire.

I think we could get near-unanimous agreement that the audit committee should be essentially independent of management. We shouldn't overreact and find ourselves with three groups of auditors: internal, public, and board of directors auditors. I think that is an invitation to compounded confusion. I will grant you, though, that the present board audit system is weak and there should be a sensible and simple way to make it more effective.

The widening concept of corporate responsibilities in social areas leads us to another facet of outside director activities. The fulfillment of corporate social responsibilities often involves expenditures of large sums of money. I am thinking of contributions to education and the staggering cost of compliance with the environmental and safety regulations. And, as Dean Brown said, it is not fair to expect top management, whose success is measured on return on investment, to deliberately take actions that increase costs without the board of directors' complete understanding and encouragement. Again, that is where experience and wide perspective of outside directors can be of help.

Still another area where we can utilize our outside directors is in consumer interface. This necessarily wouldn't apply to every company, specifically not to capital goods companies. But where you have direct contact with the consumer, then a public policy board committee is of great help. In our company only 11 percent of our total corporate sales is in the consumer area, and we are just getting into this at the board level. On the other hand, General Motors has had a public policy committee functioning on their board for the past four years.

There are five members on GM's public policy committee, all of them outside directors. Initially, I am told, they monitored the success of the equal opportunity program, as well as the corporate educational contribution program. They made suggestions for widening or rechanneling education contributions. For example, the board suggested that GM contribute substantially to research on emission standards. Then the committee began to concentrate on consumer product confidence, and that led them to an examination of the entire service and repair operation and facilities of the corporation.

Well, the outcome of that particular investigation was a suggestion by the board public policy committee that GM set up a science and advisory committee composed of five or six first-line scientists and engineers, and I am told it's been a great success. I think GM's experience with the public policy committee and this close look at consumer interface, product reliability, and product servicing, is a board activity that might well be considered by many major companies who are already involved in consumer areas or becoming more and more so.

Let me conclude with these observations.

A company can possess few more valuable assets than an active, strong, independent board of directors.

The position of all directors, but of outside directors specifically, is a crucial one in our free enterprise system. Individually and collectively, outside board members can have a profound effect on a corporation's board policy, and their widespread experience can add to the strength of any company.

Putting the Knowledge and Know-How of Outside Directors to Work

PART TWO

Bryan F. Smith

Texas Instruments, Inc.

Bryan F. Smith is an Officer of the Board and Secretary of Texas Instruments Incorporated. He was previously associated with the New York City law firm of Mitchell, Capron, Marsh, Angulo and Cooney.

Mr. Smith is a Member of the Panel on Corporate Responsibility on the Committee on Corporate Laws of the American Bar Association, a member of the New York State Bar Association, and a member of the American Society of Corporate Secretaries. He is also a member of the New York Stock Exchange Panel of Arbitrators and the Council of Financial Executives of The Conference Board.

It might shock you to hear this, but it's the view of some that directors, as they now commonly function, serve two major purposes. They satisfy the legal requirements and they provide the cover of legitimacy. If the law did not require them, they might be invented for the second purpose, which is probably most of the justification that administrators and staffs find for them now.

If indeed these directors of major institutions are largely honorary and ineffective, then they must be viewed as being not trustworthy. In fact, it might even be said that their presence may breed more distrust than if there were no trustees or directors at all. Nevertheless, in today's environment these trustees or directors have a kind of power that administrators and staffs do not have. They have the legal power to manage everything in the institution. Indeed, they have all the legal power there is. They may delegate some of it, but they can also take it back. They cannot give any of it away irretrievably and still be trustees or directors.

Those who move into a trustee's chair must be able to shift perspective, and the desire to serve should be the principal motivation for the director who would assume the power that is entrusted to him. These provocative thoughts are a paraphrase of statements by Robert Greenleaf in an essay entitled, "Trustees as Servants."

The origin of the term "outside director" is difficult to document, but it has been used for many, many years and undoubtedly began in an effort to bring some appearance of independence to the board room. The outside director traditionally spends very little time in his role, generally lending his name, prestige, and comfort to the chief executive officer, who has been responsible for his election. He is normally regarded as prestigious only if he is the chairman or president of a comparably large corporate enterprise, and thus by definition occupies a full-time high-paying job. Because of his own breadth of experience, he is able frequently to ask that disturbing or discerning question, but usually he has limited knowledge of the detailed working plans or operation of the company and, indeed, of its key people.

Nevertheless, regulatory bodies, including the New York Stock Exchange and the SEC, have strongly urged or mandated that the board should be composed of x-number of outside directors and that important committees, such as the audit committee, should have its membership from all or a majority of the outside directors.

The way to put the knowledge and know-how of outside directors to work is usually approached with the classic distinction of the outside-inside director as the overriding consideration. Roger Blough, in a very thoughtful speech to the Association of the Bar of the City of New York in February, 1973, entitled, "The Outside Director at Work on the Board," stated some guides to an outside director, including an obligation to satisfy himself with organizational structure; to pay attention to communications between management and outside directors; and to make inquiries and volunteer viewpoints rather than only to pass on questions advanced by management.

He urged that in discharging such duties the director have a certain amount of persistence, and then if unconvinced about a particular subject, to persist further until all aspects of the matter have been fully aired. He urged further that enough time be spent in actual director work, actual meeting hours, and hours outside of meeting, to have a firm overseer grasp of the corporation's business and develop an informed judgment on its more important affairs and the qualities of its officers.

These suggestions are likewise basic principles in the discussions and writings of the past two or three years on methods of improving the effectiveness of board operations, especially the effectiveness of the individual board member. The literature reveals that many of these same concerns have been critically examined at least back into the 1930's and 1940's. Remarkably, however, few basic structural or operations changes have resulted.

Although at Texas Instruments we have for many years had an active board, in 1966 we became very concerned about how we might improve its effectiveness. I have been requested in this discussion to relate the results of our study. The potential accusation of incest which Courtney Brown referred to when he and I show up on the same program might indeed be realized today. The only part which upsets me is when he appears first and I have to scramble to restate my remarks.

This morning he eloquently described a set of principles relating to membership of and operation of the board. In fact, the conclusions that TI has reached were influenced by some of the early work of Dean Brown and his subsequent thoughts. But we feel we have independently added precision and a specific case history, if you will, which puts these and other elements into practice. I thus take further issue with Dean Brown on the statement that no corporation is operating as he has suggested.

You will note that the conclusions we have reached do not distinguish between the insider and outsider, but rather stress detailed knowledge of the company and its people; the time required to understand and keep current with the company's operations and its people; also, most importantly, the independence of the individual director, be he from inside or outside the company.

An internal memo in 1966 from our chairman, P. E. Haggerty, to all TI directors was the framework for subsequent discussion and actions. It stated in part: "TI will relatively soon be a $1 billion corporation. The growth in TI's size and complexity places increasingly intensive demands on its chief operating executives and makes it difficult for such executives to spend the time necessary to study, to think quietly about, and to comprehend the importance of this rapidly changing external environment. Thus, it would seem imperative that we provide somehow at a very high level just such a thinking and deliberate comprehension of the corporation's total environment and the changing opportunities it presents. Our board represents our principal means for matching the impedances of the external and internal environments, but unless we deliberately structure our board to provide that match of external and internal environments, we are likely to drift into either a conventional outside or inside board, more likely the former.

"I suggest that several factors such as these make it desirable and necessary to do some real pioneering in the structuring of a board of directors. I think by grappling with the problem and deliberately structuring our board and its operating procedures, we can provide a badly needed coupling between the rapidly changing external and internal environments." This in 1966.

Now, as a result of our subsequent study, we have developed a written statement of policy which indicates that we will develop from within the corporation, attract from outside, and establish a flexible program of time requirements and directors' fees which will attract, develop, and retain such individuals who will comprise the TI board. In our view that policy can best be implemented by a board ranging between approximately eight and twelve members.

The fundamental principles are: In addition to the chairman and president, the TI board will be composed of general directors, officers of the board, and directors. Board members who are employees ordinarily will include only the chairman of the board, whose time commitment to TI activities may range from full-time to part-time; the president, whose time commitment to TI activities is full-time; and, on occasion, one or more officers of the board whose time commitment usually would be part-time, but in exceptional instances could be full time.

Occasionally another full-time operating officer, such as an executive vice president, may also be elected to the board, for example, during a transition period prior to his service as an officer of the board or a general director. The president is usually the chief executive officer, although the chairman could serve as such during a transition period seldom expected to exceed two or three years. The chairman of the board is usually the chief corporate officer, but only by virtue of his responsibilities as chairman of the board. As such, he might be considered not an administrator, but the professional leader of the directors, as Mr. Greenleaf has also suggested.

As chief executive officer, the president does not report to the chairman, but rather to the entire board. This is to emphasize that while the board headed by its chairman is responsible for company policies and performance, it has delegated to the company's executives headed by the chief executive officer responsibility for the detailed management of the corporation.

Most board members will be general directors. They are not employees of TI, although they may have been in the past, and must assume board duties, including membership on committees, chairmanship of committees, and optional additional activities in TI's interests, with a minimum time commitment of approximately 30 days per year. While the basic time commitment for a general director is a minimum of approximately 30 days, depending upon need, availability, and interest, it could be 40, 60, 80, or in unusual circumstances even more days. His compensation will vary accordingly.

Currently, there are seven general directors. Two were previously officers of the board and TI employees. Approximately one year ago they retired as active employees under the retirement policy I will describe later and were then elected general directors. One, Erik Jonsson, was a founder of TI in 1930 and retired as chairman of the board in 1966. He is also our honorary chairman. The remaining four are outsiders in the conventional sense.

Officer of the board was formerly the title for general directors, but now it is reserved for a board member who is an employee other than the chairman or president and who also devotes principal amounts of his time to his duties as a director. The other category is director. Ordinarily, there will be not more than two or three persons serving in this category. They are available for scheduled board meetings and activities and for limited committee duties. Such directors could be individuals with little or no previous TI association, but usually already will have an intimate knowledge from prior TI association.

Directors in this category are expected to spend 15 days per year on TI business. Now, a primary consideration in selecting an individual as a general director, director, or officer of the board, is his ability to bring to the board a dispassionate point of view. Although the general director, director, or officer of the board whose working experience has been largely within TI may be an objective individual, it is only reasonable to expect that his long experience in the TI culture, where personal commitment to goals is strongly emphasized, would tend to develop some strong personal bias. To assist such a board member to develop and maintain a more dispassionate perspective toward TI, the selection of an individual as a board member and his acceptance anticipates that he will enter into activities outside of TI which will supplement his experience in a meaningful way.

Such activities should expose him to environments in which a diversity of viewpoints would be expressed, where the performance of individuals in quite different endeavors from our own company's may require evaluation, and possibly where some of the approaches developed in TI might be tried and further evaluated. A written statement of policy describes the functioning of the board and its committees. Among other things, it states it is a basic policy of our board to organize the use of directors' time to insure that they are always adequately knowledgeable about TI plans, operations, and performance.

The activities of the board include, of course, attendance at monthly and special board meetings, attendance at corporate planning meetings, and occasional visits to TI plant and office locations. However, in determining the appropriate amount of time to be spent in such activities, careful organization is required. To assure a desired coupling between the board and the organization, TI expects most board members to attend at least some of the scheduled operating organizational meetings, internally known as quarterly financial reviews. These are reviews of activities in process and performance of product groups and are held quarterly by the appropriate operating organization.

Attendance by directors at such reviews provides the opportunity to become acquainted with key TI personnel, their operations, and the environments in which they must succeed. In addition to the expected attendance at the strategic planning conference, which is held in the spring of each year and lasts three to four days, the directors are encouraged and have received the full cooperation of the management to discuss informally outside of normal board or committee meetings specific items of interest, such as product development, marketing, or financial matters.

Obviously, if this is carried to extremes, it can have a disrupting effect on management; but it has been found in experimenting with the policy for the last two years that we have been able to achieve an appropriate balance from both sides, which in turn has been a very useful and constructive interchange. One of our outside directors, commenting on his board experience, said the following: "I have served on the TI board for more than four years as an 'outside' member," not a general director. "I put the word 'outside' in quotes because it is commonly used for a person of my type who is not an employee and usually is also not a former employee. Yet I find that the word is not representative of my situation. I don't feel like an outsider, I am not treated like one, and yet it is clear to everyone in the company and to me that I am not subject to the company's discipline and pressures for conformity. On the contrary, the pressures are all directed toward increasing my detailed knowledge of the company's operations."

"As an 'outsider-insider' I have always felt that my ideas were not only welcome, but were continuously solicited. To put all of the above in a succinct form, TI has changed the board's right to know into the director's duty to know." Another outside director said: "Perhaps the outstanding feature is that the main thrust of the board's work is not carried on through an executive committee, but through the work of the board itself. The psychological rewards derived from the in-depth involvement permitted by service on the board are correspondingly great. Such rewards are quite apart from monetary compensation or professional enlightenment, but derive very directly from the feeling that one is a genuine part of the team and that one's comments and opinions are not merely respected, but are sought out as essential ingredients in the formation of policy."

The participation of the outside director on committees is also an important factor in putting his knowledge and know-how to work. I agree with Mr. Rockwell that outsiders do make important contributions on compensation committees as well as in other committee roles if they put the time into it. Committee assignments are reviewed by us at least annually and provide an opportunity for change if desirable. It also provides a review of the time which board members spend on board matters and in turn the basis for determining their individual compensation.

Now, if we are able to retain and attract competent directors, it is of great importance to provide compensation beyond the conventional few hundred dollar fee per meeting that most directors receive. General directors in our case, that is those who commit to approximately 30 days per year, including attendance at board and planning meetings and committee assignments, will be paid at the basic rate of $30,000, a rate comparable to that charged by consultants when serving corporate clients. In addition, if more days of service are required, and agreement with the individual director is reached, a fee structure has been established that goes beyond the basic rate for general directors and which is computed by relating such fees to the compensation of the key officers of the company.

For those directors whose responsibilities include minimum attendance at monthly board meetings and annual planning meeting, for a total of approximately 15 days per year, the fee is $15,000 per year. In evolving these principles and recognizing the scope of our long-range development programs, several vital concerns became more obvious.

Not only must the organization possess a completely adequate staff of managers currently, but it must have available a succession of competent and trained individuals for the years ahead. A corrollary and primary concern for both the board of directors and the company's top management is the need to provide the maximum opportunity for all TI'ers throughout the world to realize their desired potential.

As key steps in meeting these two vital concerns, in 1973 we adopted an early retirement policy that covers the chairman, president, executive vice presidents, and officers of the board. Briefly stated, the chairman and president must retire at 62, but may retire as early as 55. Executive vice presidents are expected usually to retire at 55. This is the mandatory age for officers of the board. These policies mean that ordinarily TI's executive vice presidents will not be older than 52, and usually younger, when they are elected. A president will normally not be more than 50 at the time of his election.

One of the principles related to the election of officers of the board is to encourage them to develop a dispassionate interest and independent view of TI's operations. We, therefore, adopted additional policies to help them become independent in their judgment, including retirement at 55. This early retirement, however, is not intended to preclude their continued service as a director, most likely as a general director, but rather to encourage and emphasize the independent viewpoint expected by terminating their previous employment and thus breaking sharply their relationship, both subordinate and superior, with TI executives.

In this I take issue with the remarks of Mr. Lewis this morning. Obviously, there is also great value to the corporation in retaining men with years of experience as executives with TI. There are other aspects of our experience which time does not permit me to go into, but I do not presume to suggest that we have the ideal solution.

What we have added is more precision to the distinction between the board and operating management; more emphasis on the time required to perform the board job; a pattern of compensation for board members which recognizes the value of their time commitment; and a definite emphasis on objective and independent viewpoints of the individual board member.

A primary objective of the board of directors today is to assure the continuity and self-renewal of the corporation. If so, it is not important whether the individual director is an outsider or insider, but whether he is independent not of the company, but of the management of the company. In line with Mr. Rockwell's remarks, I suggest that the classic distinction between outsider and insider be replaced by a distinction between the director and the top manager.

Dean Brown, in a 1974 essay entitled, "Legitimacy, Objectivity, and Vitality of the Board of Directors of the Large Company," has succinctly stated it as follows: "One basic reason for the shortcomings of boards of directors is that their functions have not been clearly defined and, especially, kept separate from those of the management. It seems to me that a very important step in strengthening the position and role of the board is to make sure that it is separate from management, both in function and in manning."

Now, we believe our approaches to assuring the independence of directors whose work experience has been primarily within the company, and which normally would cause them to be classified as insiders, are appropriate in that they assure the presence of directors with broad previous experience in the complex management of the company, while at the same time enhancing their independence by requiring retirement at 55 and encouraging auxiliary non-TI activities to assure a broadened and more critical viewpoint. Outsiders bring to the board, it is certainly true, a very useful and valuable dimension and balance in the constructive sense.

Finally, one anticipatory remark to the expected message from the Chairman of the SEC on standards of conduct and how changes should be brought about. It is suggested simply that it is highly undesirable to have change directed through government action, be they SEC guidelines or otherwise, as opposed to self-initiated improvement by corporate boards. I hope that we will not simply perpetuate the re-examination of the same old subjects and the same old cliches, but on the contrary, will undertake serious re-examination of our respective boards, their operation, membership, and effectiveness, and undertake serious steps to put to work the knowledge and know-how not only of outside directors, but of all interested parties in endeavoring to improve them.

Question: As I am a long-time stockholder in your company, Rockwell International, I am concerned about two things about your board operation: 1) the full board meets only quarterly; 2) your executive committee meets more regularly, but it is totally made up of insiders. How do you feel you get enough outside look in your position with all subordinates on your executive committee?

Mr. Rockwell: Well, first I should ask if John Gilbert is here, because for three years he has put a vote to our stockholders that we should have at least 10 board meetings a year. I don't see that we need 10 board meetings per year. We give our directors every month very full and complete financial statements and other data about the company. At our quarterly meetings we give them a very thorough financial review. We meet generally at a plant location in order to give them a picture of what we are doing in a particular area, and generally have dinner the night before and then bring in the management of that plant, let them explain their operation to the directors, and review their operations for them. The next day we spend an hour or two in the plant actually looking at what they told about the night before. The rest of the day is involved with the meeting.

We are probably holding two extra meetings this year, one to discuss the subject of the social responsibility of the corporation and probably another one on strategy.

At our meetings we outline the strategy for each of our five divisions of the corporation. We do the financial allocation, resources allocation, and the other things that boards have to approve. Our inside executive committee I find a very handy thing because it isn't delegated too many things except perhaps the routine matters that have to be taken care of between board meetings; and these are reported to the board immediately when we take action on them and, as I say, they are relatively limited. We don't have to call the board more often than four or five or maybe six times a year.

And let me tell you if you want to lose some board member, just go from four or five or six times a year to 12 times. I had to leave one board because I just couldn't spend the time on it. Another good example is our audit committee. We have three directors on our audit committee, and they asked us to add two more directors because they couldn't get a quorum. They are busy people, and it is difficult to get all three of those members of the audit committee together to do the job the audit committee is required to do.

Question: Bryan, what is the mandatory retirement age of outside directors? How does the executive vice president feel about leaving the arena of day-to-day action at age 55?

Mr. Smith: Well, first, mandatory retirement age for outside directors is 70, with the exception of our two remaining founder directors, where the mandatory age is 75.

Both of those gentlemen are in between 70 and 75, so that in a couple of years they will have retired under that policy. Second point, it was a matter of some concern as to what the reaction might be not only of the executive vice president currently in the incumbent spot, but also those fellows who might look forward to occupying that chair, to the adoption of 55 as the mandatory early retirement age. And I might say that we originally started out feeling that 60 was an appropriate age rather than 55.

When we looked at it, however, in the context of at least several of those kinds of people being very important and serious candidates for either officer of the board slots or general director spots of the kind that I described, we began to feel that the very important factor was in creating an atmosphere and doing something that was very concrete with teeth in it that added to this idea of independence of the individual board member, particularly those who would come from the inside.

Given all these things, we went forward with the 55, and I must say that the acceptance of the policy was universal among the younger managers, including the three executive vice presidents. And it's been a very rewarding kind of thing and what it did, in addition, was it opened up over the course of the next 10 to 15 years about three times as many promotion opportunities than would have existed under the other more normal retirement policy. And I think this was really the clincher because the young fellows really did see that.

Question: If an executive vice president retires at 55, which he must, how is his pension determined compared to age 65 and does he automatically become a member of the board at that time?

Mr. Smith: On the latter point, he does not automatically become a member of the board. He must be selected as a candidate and elected. So that it is not automatic, although I think it is our feeling that because of the quality of the people, there are several executive vice presidents who will become board members. On the matter of the calculation of pensions, in the interest of time I did not describe the way in which that is handled.

In addition to his normal discounted pension benefit, which is fully vested at 55, we have adopted what we call a supplementary retirement scheme which tries to take into account at least a portion of the financial burden that the man obviously would suffer if he just did nothing else. And that benefit is calculated by extending his salary rate into the future until age 65 and then discounted back to 65 and added on top of his normal benefit. So that there is an extra element of compensation through a scheme which is added.

Question: Bryan, exactly what does an "officer of the board" do compared to the others?

Mr. Smith: I have been in that slot now for two years and I have spent all of my time on board-related matters. I do not have any operating responsibilities as such, and a great portion of that time has been spent in working with the chairman and two general directors, in an administrative committee of our board which developed for presentation to the full board the set of principles which I described on the board's operation, the early retirement policy, and all of the things associated with it.

I continue as secretary to the board and act either as secretary or as a consultant to the committees of the board, including the compensation committee. And I am the chairman of the audit committee, and the trust investment committee, which supervises the investments of our pension and retirement funds.

Performance Audits
by Outside Directors

Harold Byron Smith, Jr.

Illinois Tool Works, Inc.

Harold Byron Smith, Jr. is President of Illinois Tool Works, Inc. Additionally, he is a Director of the First National Bank & Trust Company of Barrington, a Director of the Skil Corporation, the Marshall Field Company, the Northern Trust Company, and the Illinois Manufacturers' Association. He is also a Trustee of Northwestern Mutual Life Insurance Company.

Mr. Smith has been active in many civic, cultural and educational organizations. He serves as a Trustee and Vice President of the Adler Planetarium, a Trustee of the Chicago Historical Society; the Council for Technological Advancement; the Newberry Library; Northwestern University; and the Rush-Presbyterian-St. Luke's Medical Center.

A performance audit by outside directors is one specific technique proposed to help meet the challenge of new roles, rules, and responsibilities of corporate directors. At this point it is difficult to analyze empirically the potential value and viability of a performance audit technique. There is little practical experience from which judgments can be drawn. And the technique is sufficiently different from the usually accepted working relationship between a board and management to warrant close examination before adoption.

In this discussion, I'd like to first position the performance audit within the broader spectrum of possible director activities; then examine one specific proposal which describes what a performance audit would be and how it might be undertaken; review some parallels on what may shed some light on the performance of an audit; and then add some observations.

I should state at the outset the personal view that there is a fundamental distinction between the roles of directors and managers which should be preserved and that neither role can be well executed unless that distinction is recognized. The observations and conclusions I offer are admittedly reflective of that bias.

The continuing discussion of the appropriate degree and kind of outside director participation arises from two basic concerns. On the one hand it is occasioned by new interpretations of liability. Enough horror stories abound to arouse the interest of anyone serving as a director; and regulatory bodies, both public and private, are increasingly defining, or trying to define, what these liabilities are.

In the second sense, however, the discussion also arises from a continuing review as to what role outside directors can or should play in guiding as well as reviewing the conduct of the management of the enterprise; from an exploration of ways in which outside directors might become contributing participants rather than passive overseers ratifying management decisions and assuming a truly active role only in emergencies.

The evolution of the typical board committee structure can be viewed as a response to both of these factors: minimizing liability and increasing participation. The recent increase in the use of audit committees is an example. A Conference Board survey of a large sample of both manufacturing and non-manufacturing companies showed that audit committees are now established in 45 percent of the 853 businesses examined, about double the proportion in a similar study five years ago.

The audit committees are, in many cases, involved not only in overseeing the annual audit, but also extending their work to provide outside directors the opportunity to participate in consideration of accounting policies in general. Similarly, compensation committees, also increasing in popularity, may expand their activities beyond compensation matters to include an evaluation of management and organization structure and staffing.

Other common committee designations include finance, pension, contribution, investment, public policy, and so forth. Each offers some opportunity for director involvement, but in the main the tasks which define board committees are oriented toward matters that legally or by tradition require board action and are thus extensions of what is customarily thought to be the work of the board.

The performance audit concept is a departure from that orientation, extending outside board member involvement actively into areas previously considered by some to be the responsibility of management. It is not just an extension of traditional board functions, but a new role and one creating a new relationship between a board and its management. This distinction becomes clear in considering one approach to performance audits described by Frazier Wilde and Richard Vancil in an article which appeared in 1972 in the *Harvard Business Review.*

They defined a performance audit as an independent appraisal of management performance by a formally constituted non-management group—in the typical corporate situation, outside directors. It is not an audit in a financial sense. While it may involve quantitative evaluation, the real interest is qualitative judgment on performance and outlook. The audit is initiated or agreed to by management, authorized by the full board, and administered by a subcommittee of outside directors who are empowered to obtain whatever internal or external assistance they require.

The nominal purpose of the audit is to appraise results so the board can knowledgeably evaluate strategy and objectives which management proposes. The real purpose, in their view, is to create an informed dialogue between the president and his directors about future performance standards for which the president will subsequently be held accountable by the board.

The development of these performance standards is the first specific objective of the audit. The writers suggest these standards go beyond such measures as earnings per share or growth rates. They should be expressed in terms relative to the external environment in which the company operates: market share, technological posture, return on capital relative to competitors, and so forth. The standards should include those areas which management has identified as critical factors for success. As a result of the audit, the board should understand why these factors are strategically important, how management can act to effect results, and what action management proposes.

The second objective of the performance audit as proposed is an evaluation of the quality of management both individually and collectively, and the quality of the management process. Here the suggestion is that outside directors undertaking a performance audit can collectively form judgments about the management group by direct contact with a cross-section of executives as part of the audit process.

The third objective is an appraisal of the quality of corporate citizenship. In this area, they suggest outside directors may have an advantage over management, particularly if the board has been chosen to provide diversity of background and perspective. Attention should be devoted not only to current issues, but should look ahead, evaluating corporate objectives and strategies against the social and political backgrounds likely to exist in the future. The writer suggests that the audit not be an annual exercise. Too frequent use of the audit process would not only be burdensome, but would risk introducing a short-term perspective. Typically, the audit might have a three to five year horizon.

In summary, then, the performance audit as proposed has three basic objectives: understanding and appraising key strategies and objectives and agreeing with management on performance standards; 2) evaluating the quality of management and the management process; and 3) viewing the business against present and emerging social and political backgrounds. It is presumed that the audit could result in recommendations to the full board for action.

This proposal stops short of suggesting specific methodology for undertaking a performance audit. Depending on the size and diversity of the business, the approach can be relatively simple or extensive and complex. But two important conditions are implicit in whatever approach might be taken: outside directors would become systematically involved in the consideration and evaluation of strategic alternatives and planning; and to properly perform the audit, outside directors could be obliged to seek non-management sources of information to confirm to their independent satisfaction questions of judgment.

Evidence demonstrating the practicality of the performance audit technique in actual use is sparse. Obviously, the kinds of tasks constituting an audit as proposed are undertaken on an ad hoc basis by directors in times of corporate crisis. But examples of regular, formalized performance audits, if they do exist, are not widely reported.

There are examples, sometimes referenced, which come close, however. The Northwestern Mutual Life Insurance Company policyowner examining committee is a long established example that closely parallels a performance audit. Its roots go back to the earliest days of the company when a committee of three board members—not members of the executive committee—were charged with independently examining the company's affairs from time to time and reporting their findings to the entire board.

In the early 1900's the composition of the committee was changed to five policyowners not otherwise associated with the company. Today the committee's charter by resolution of the board reads in part as follows: "The examining committee shall each year make an investigation of and inquire into the general policies, operations, and management of the company in such a manner as it may determine, with authority to employ at the expense of the company and under the sole direction and supervision of the committee such assistance as it may deem advisable, and to report to the board on the results of the committee's investigation."

In addition, the committee's formal report is included in the company's annual report sent to all policyowners, receiving space comparable to that devoted to the president's letter. Prospective members of this committee are recommended by the company's agents and others, screened by the top management, and staff, invited to serve by the president, and elected by the board. Efforts are made to assure that most members of each year's committee have had experience with major enterprises. The past five committees have included 10 chief executives and five senior officers of other companies, six professional people, two economists, one university administrator, and one rancher. Thus, in background the composition of the committee is not dissimilar to a group of outside directors of another corporation.

Typically, this committee meets for six or more working days over a period of two or three months at the company's home office. Interviews are held with all executive officers, with concentration at the senior level. Others such as agents, the outside auditors, outside legal counsel, and company people, in addition to executive officers, are frequently interviewed. All the records of the company are available to the committee and outside consultants have on occasion been employed.

While there is no prescribed format for the committee's work, it is interesting to observe that the examination has nearly always gravitated to the subject matter proposed for a performance audit. Objectives and strategies are examined and evaluated. A consensus appraisal of the character and quality of management and the management process tends to emerge even with relatively brief exposure. And questions of public policy and corporate citizenship are considered.

The report of the committee to the board usually covers each of these areas. Conclusions and recommendations sometimes reinforce existing management's point of view and sometimes result in new courses of action. One committee in the early thirties noted that record keeping was handled in each department and recommended the establishment of a centralized office of the controller, a recommendation promptly adopted.

Another committee explored the changing character of the policyowners, requested an in-depth study by outside consultants, and the result was a major revamping of the company's advertising. Compensation policy and organization structure and staffing, including top management succession, have received attention. A recent committee, concerned with changing conditions in the insurance market and new thrusts of public policy, urged formation of a corporate long-range planning function responsible directly to the president.

The NML experience, while not an exact parallel to the performance audit as proposed, nevertheless sheds some light on the potential of the concept for other organizations. First, the exercise is credited with contributions to the success of the business. While it cannot be claimed that the recommendations of the committee would not have otherwise been considered and implemented by management, it is clear that some important management actions have been generated or encouraged by the committee. Beyond the identifiable contributions, however, management believes that the activities of the committee in making its examination have a constructive effect on the organization.

Second, the NML experience demonstrates the value to an outsider of participating in the audit process to build a reference base for use in future evaluation of management's performance. While the NML examining committee members are not board members, new directors are frequently selected from past committee members. Those who do become directors, now 17 out of 30, look upon the examining committee experience as a foundation for exercising their role that would be difficult to duplicate otherwise.

Finally, the NML experience demonstrates that the process need not necessarily impair the important distinction between directing and managing the business. In this regard, however, the NML situation must be considered in light of some special circumstances. The examining committee has a history nearly as long as the company itself and successive management teams have grown up in an organization framework accustomed to its work. It is a unique institution which the company management regards as an asset. Further, examining committee members are not board members and while their influence can be substantial, their tenure is limited. Taking all this into account, the NML success could be argued to be a special case and not typical of what other companies would experience if they chose to initiate a similar exercise.

A second and somewhat different application of the concept of performance audit is represented in the establishment just this year of a public review board by Arthur Andersen & Company. In announcing its creation, Arthur Andersen said its board will review the professional operations of the firm, including the way it is managed and financed, the scope of its practice, how the quality of the work is controlled, and performance related to the public interest, a statement that includes all the objectives of a performance audit customized to the function of a public accounting firm.

This board has five members of diverse backgrounds, but with important business and academic credentials. The board may establish its own program and have whatever staff assistance it considers necessary, may visit any office of the firm, and interview any personnel.

The board is expected to devote substantial time to its work, 15 to 20 days each year. It is empowered to make comments and suggestions to management of improvements that in its judgment should be considered, and to prepare an annual report to be published by the firm. However, it has no responsibility for making or implementing policies or procedures. The role and responsibility of management and the inside board of directors is preserved.

The work of the board is just getting off the ground and as experience accumulates it may shed some light on the practical application of performance audit techniques. But this example also involves special circumstances. As a partnership, AA's options in introducing involvement by outsiders are limited. A panel such as that established may have been set up because it was the only practical way to obtain outside participation which the firm thought useful. And here again, similar to the NML situation, the review board members are not directors and play an exclusively advisory role.

A third and final example of a proposal along the lines of a performance audit was offered by Arthur Goldberg in the incident that led to his resignation from the board of directors of TWA. Expressing the view that he could not otherwise perform the legal obligations of an outside director, he proposed the establishment of a committee of overseers composed exclusively of outside directors.

To quote from his proposals: "Such a committee would be generally responsible for supervising company operations on a broad scale and make periodic reports to the board. To perform these duties adequately, this committee would need authorization to hire a small staff of experts who would be responsible only to the board and would be totally independent of management control. In addition, the committee should also be empowered to engage the services of consultants of the highest competence.

"As the eyes and ears of the directors, these independent experts and their staff assistants and consultants would look into major policy questions and report to the committee, and through them to the board as a whole, before decisions are taken on management recommendations. The fundamental responsibility of these experts, staff, and consultants would be to provide an independent source of expertise for the board. This would enable the board members to fulfill the due diligence requirements of a reasonable, independent investigation of company operations."

Clearly this proposal goes beyond the limitations suggested for performance audits. The committee of overseers and its staff would be a continuing rather than an occasional activity. It would operate totally independent of management, yet have substantial, if not overriding, influence on the board, It is difficult for me to visualize how any management could work effectively under such circumstances. The example is useful if only to emphasize the problems that could arise should the performance audit concept be carried to an illogical extreme.

The risk of destroying the fundamental distinction between directing and managing becomes the pivotal question in considering performance audits. It is difficult to argue that the objectives of the audit should not be satisfied by some mechanism involving board members and management. Directors should have an understanding of the strategies and objectives of the business, have confidence that they are soundly conceived, and be able to appraise performance. They should be able to evaluate the quality of management and management process and should bring their perspective to bear on reconciling the conduct of business with society at large. If achieving these objectives through the performance audit technique presents other and new problems, however, then alternative methods ought to be considered first.

A redefinition of the tasks of the standing board committees is one possible. The General Electric approach is a case in point. Committees of the board include management development and compensation, audit and finance, operations, technology and science, and public issues, each an area identified jointly by the board and management as one in which outside director understanding and involvement is appropriate and important. Each committee is chaired by an outside director. Each outside director serves on two committees, and each committee is constituted to have a director from each of the other committees. Committee meetings are regularly scheduled with agendas and reports. They involve direct contact with department managers, division managers, and group executives, providing an opportunity for inquiry, understanding, and involvement.

In the hands of directors and managers intent on making it work, such a committee setup seems capable of satisfying the needs of directors envisaged in a performance audit. And, I suspect, there are many other examples of structures carefully designed to fit the needs of other companies. TI is an example we just heard.

A statement attributed to M. J. Rathbone, former chairman of Standard Oil, sums up well the issue that must be faced by those considering or advocating the performance audit technique: "A man who is in a tough executive post has got to be able to call together a group of his associates, his colleagues, his subordinates, and sound out his plans, thrash them out when they are in half-baked form. But in addition, I believe very strongly that he needs one more step if you are going to have the proper safeguards, and that is the job of proving his point to an independent group that are damn good judges who have not been participants in the plans, but who stand aside and judge. They interfere in no way with management, but they are judges. I think if that element is lacking, you are always in danger. Any chief executive should have the full authority, but also should have that privilege of going before a board and defending his practice.''

If one subscribes to that point of view, then the performance audit technique should be considered only in a situation where both management and directors are convinced that the process will not threaten either the authority of management or the independent judgment of directors. If either of these essentials could be at risk, they should seek other means of informing and involving outside directors.

Question: This is for Harold Smith. Would it be better to have the standing audit committee make any performance audits? Standing audit committee as distinct from the performance audit committee.

Mr. Harold Smith: If you accept the definition of a performance audit as I have seen it in the literature, it goes way beyond anything that's been suggested by the standing audit committee. Now, you could have a standing audit committee do it on the presumption that it was composed exclusively of outside directors and would be a logical group to assign the task. But it should be understood that the scope here is far broader and more deeply involved in management activities, in planning, in participation, in strategic planning, than anything I have seen or heard about in terms of the conventional committee structure.

Question: Harold, what is the difference between a) the conduct of a performance and b) those things which the board should be concerned about in its normal ongoing role?

Mr. Harold Smith: I don't think there is very much difference. It is a question of how you go about doing it. And the element in the performance audit is that the outside directors as an independent group looking to resources other than management systematically move through the organization making their own independent interpretations. Now, that's a far different thing than the kinds of things we described otherwise in both the two previous presentations and I think there probably are many variations on that theme, where the objective can be accomplished by using a technique that maintains the distinction between manager and director.

Question: Harold, if outside auditors such as Arthur Andersen conduct a management performance review, how can they maintain objectivity in the audit function if their management performance review recommendations are implemented?

Mr. Harold Smith: I think that's a real problem. Are some of the accounting firms suggesting that that is a proper way?

Mr. Mueller: Yes, they have a bias in that regard.

Mr. Harold Smith: I don't think we can do it. It seems to me that it does set up a conflict. I think the independence of the auditors is a key thing and they ought to stay otherwise uninvolved. It wouldn't be unlike the point made this morning of having a member of your outside accounting firm on your board of directors. You are coming pretty close to that kind of a relationship.

Question: Mr. Rockwell, do you or Bryan want to comment on that, outside auditors conducting a management performance review? How can they maintain objectivity?

Mr. Rockwell: I think it would be pretty difficult. I certainly wouldn't want our outside auditors to be performing a management audit review in addition to their function as auditors.

Mr. Bryan Smith: In the context of the question, if I understand it, as to what the question means by management performance review, I think it is completely inappropriate for the outside auditors to do that; in contrast to their very normal practice of commenting on the strength of the internal controls, the quality of the financial staff, and things of that nature. On the other hand, the management performance review in most places where there is an effective compensation committee or personnel evaluation committee is indeed handled very competently and conscientiously by such a committee.

Board Membership Accountability and Responsibility: What Labor Expects

I. W. Abel

United Steelworkers of America

I. W. Abel is the International President of the United Steelworkers of America. He is also President of the Industrial Union Department (IUD) of the AFL–CIO, and a Vice President of the national AFL–CIO.

Mr. Abel has served on various boards and commissions, both Government and private. He was a member of President Johnson's National Management Advisory Committee, and the National Advisory Commission on Civil Disorders established after the 1967 disorders in the nation's cities. In 1969 Mr. Abel was named a member of the General Advisory Committee on Arms Control and Disarmament and a member of the President's Task Force on Air Pollution. In 1971, Mr. Abel was appointed to the Pay Board under the Stabilization Program. He, and the other two AFL–CIO members on the Board, resigned from the Board in 1972 in protest against its policies. In 1973, he was named a member of the Labor-Management Advisory Committee to the Cost of Living Council under Phase II of the President's wage-price control program.

I suppose you have noticed that the manner in which Americans use or misuse the English language is constantly changing. New expressions or phrases come in vogue such as: "At this point in time," "stonewalling," or "scenario," not to overlook "input." Now, some would say I was here to give this conference some input from organized labor, and this is a welcome change because usually the other side of the table is more interested in talking to labor about output. Surprisingly enough, I will have a few words to say about output in the course of my remarks.

I am flattered by the invitation to speak because I certainly do not pretend to be an expert nor have special knowledge in the field of corporate directorships. I have sat on the boards of the United Steelworkers of America and that of the AFL–CIO, but my knowledge about corporate boards of directors is limited in a sense. I am told that in the past corporate directors were chosen primarily because they were important community figures or because big names in the world of business and education gave prestige to the corporation. Occasionally corporate membership provided an appearance of hard work for the college drop-out, son-in-law of the president of the corporation.

Until recently there seemed to be a feeling that directors were rather superfluous people. This was my attitude, perhaps, but certainly these misconceptions about directors and corporations are changing. Directors may not have been very important people to American corporations at one time, but it seems to me that they are becoming more and more important. Recently there has been evidence of this from many sources. I have read of conscientious efforts to obtain corporate directors to represent the consumers' point of view and the view of the minority citizens, and that is to the good.

Business Week Magazine on November 23, 1974, carried an article warning corporate directors their job is no longer a sinecure. It stated, and I quote: "You are committing yourselves to spending plenty of hours on company problems." And the article in *Business Week* went on to warn potential directors that they not only have to work hard for the corporation, but they will also face the possibility of being sued for wrong decisions by disgruntled stockholders and others, including the Securities and Exchange Commission. We live in a world of emerging Watergate mentality and it is evident that the public rightfully expects not only conduct that is legal, but also ethical. *Business Week* thus underlines the increasing importance of the boards of directors to corporations.

This conference, with all of its distinguished participants, is another indication of the increasing role of the corporate director. I do believe that corporations as such have an increasing sense of social accountability beyond that of simple profit making. They are realizing they are part of a greater American community and they will be held to account for their actions. Corporate directors are participants in the day-to-day management of their enterprises and must share in the end result of good or bad programming and achievement in the field of social accountability.

Therefore, we should examine the responsibility of directors in terms of their larger responsibility to the corporations themselves. Just how tremendous this power of corporate America has grown was indicated in the May issue of *Fortune* magazine. In its annual study of corporate power concentration, *Fortune* pointed out that the 500 largest industrials now account for 65 percent of the sales of all U.S. industrial corporations, 76 percent of the employees, and 79 percent of the profits. In terms of employment, these 500 companies are listed as employing more than 15 million workers. The amount of their sales combined exceeds two-thirds of a trillion dollars. Their profits are close to $39 billion. In 1973, to which these figures apply, their sales increased almost 20 percent and their profits increased 39 percent over the previous year.

Now, I think it is evident from these figures that those of you who sit in the corporate board rooms and advise managers have an incredible responsibility because your influence on corporate operations represents such a vast part of the private enterprise system and corporate activities within that system. But even in the smaller corporate enterprise, manufacturing or financial, certainly the directors have a role of great responsibliity.

We might identify these responsibilities in four generalized categories. These might well be as follows: No. 1, the attitudes of the corporations toward their workers. No. 2, their attitudes toward consumers. No. 3, the corporation's attitudes toward local and national governments, or the national scene. And No. 4, the responsibilities of corporations in an international frame of reference.

Now, I would like to expand somewhat on each of these four responsibilities. First, the attitude of the directors and the management of corporations toward their workers.

Workers have a basic right under the law of this nation to select a union of their choice and to engage in collective bargaining concerning their working conditions, wages, and benefits. It is the responsibility of the corporation management, buttressed by pressure from the directors, if you please, to see that the corporation does not interfere with this basic legal right and to bargain in good faith with the union which the workers have chosen.

There should be good-faith bargaining not only on wages, working conditions, and benefits, but on the whole area of job security, safety, seniority, and retirement security after one is too old to work and yet still too young to die. There is also the question of job satisfaction, and the right of workers to work with a sense of dignity to the degree possible, with the enthusiasm that comes when one works at a job in which he has interest and a sense of creating something worthwhile. There also is the potential partnership role that can grow out of common endeavors with management.

This thought of the potential partnership role is not new as far as the United Steelworkers of America is concerned. It may surprise some of you, but even before he became the first and founding president of our union, Philip Murray was thinking and writing along these lines more than 30 years ago. In 1940, when he was chairman of the Steelworkers Organizing Committee as well as vice president of the United Mine Workers of America, Phil Murray co-authored a book titled, *Organized Labor and Production.*

And I would like to quote a few paragraphs from a chapter in the book called, "Tapping Labor's Brains." This is what Phil Murray wrote in that chapter some 34 years ago. He said, "When the early union contracts were being signed, workers often expressed a desire to cooperate with management in improving the business. These proffers were discouraged by management on the theory that headwork was the prerogative of the white collar folk. Though there has been some change in this attitude, even today there is all too much emphasis on the traditional barriers between management and men. And this in spite of the fact that during the last 50 years scientific management has made it clear that only through close cooperation between workers and employers can maximum production be secured.

"Now," Murray wrote, "as management and labor through strong labor unions become more nearly equal in bargaining power, they can either wage war to gain the spoils of production restriction, or they can together devise improved production practices that increase social income. The second course is more in keeping with the potential age of plenty. Further, it opens up vast opportunities for democratic experience. For organized workers to come face to face with management's problems will have both an educational and sobering influence, just as management will be both educated and sobered by insight into the problems of unions.

"Power, wherever it lies," Mr. Murray continued, "cannot in the long run be disassociated from responsibility. If the labor movement fails to develop an adequate sense of responsibility for output, the alternative will be increasing tension and bitterness over wages, hours, and working conditions, reducing the opportunity for constructive accommodation and community of interest between management and union."

"Speaking generally," and these are still Phil Murray's words, "the developing attitude of industry toward its personnel may be divided into four phases: 1) a condition that is paternalistic and ununionized; 2) the struggle for unionization ending in recognition, collective bargaining, and a written contract; 3) a gradual strengthening in contractual relations and continued efforts toward improvement in hours, wages, and working conditions; and 4) the beginnings of labor-management collaboration for greater gross productivity in which both may share, thereby affording organized labor the fullest status and widest hearing consistent with unified direction and control of the enterprise."

"During the first three of these phases, a decidedly militaristic type of leadership is dominant. Only as American industry enters the fourth state, represented today by a few spearhead enterprises, will there be a demand for labor leaders who are production conscious and who are ready and able to cooperate with management in furthering the common enterprise." So wrote Phil Murray in 1940.

Now, it is interesting to note that what Phil Murray wrote in 1940 came to pass in 1971 in our union negotiations with the nation's major basic steel companies. Perhaps some of you here today recall that in those negotiations there was included in the final settlement a provision that established a joint advisory committee at each plant of the industry to devise ways and means of imrpoving productivity and promoting the use of domestic steel. Of course, we made it clear that such a provision did not affect wages, working conditions, rights and benefits by contract.

We also made it clear that we weren't talking about reductions in crew sizes, job eliminations, job combinations, or work speed-ups. It was stressed that the joint effort would be carried out in the spirit of good will, with common concern for each other's interests. What we were talking about was the use of modern technology, better tools and equipment, working smarter, worker effectiveness, elimination of waste, improving safety experience and employee morale, reducing equipment breakdowns, etc.

Both sides agreed to the provision on productivity and promoting the use of basic steel because of the threat of steel imports on the industry and our members and the flooding of this country with other imports, produced by exploited labor abroad, that was costing thousands and thousands of American jobs in this counrty.

Now, shortly after the productivity clause was made a part of the 1971 settlement, a joint union-industry conference on imports and productivity was held in this very hotel. At that conference I urged the company officials to seek the suggestions and advice of our members on productivity because I assured them our members had much to contribute. "You may find it hard to believe," I told them, "but they can teach you a thing or two in the interests of all of us." Well, the joint plant committees on productivity, under guidelines set up by a top level joint union-industry committee, were established and started to function late in 1972 and throughout 1973. The annual productivity increase in the American steel industry since 1965 had been the lowest of any free world nation.

So we had our work cut out for us. But we were successful. On June 11th of this year, the U.S. Labor Department's Bureau of Labor Statistics announced that steel was the one major industry that had a significant increase in productivity last year over the previous year. It said productivity in the steel industry increased 10.8 percent in 1973, compared with 5.8 percent in '72, nearly a 100 percent increase. The Bureau also announced that steel output increased 19 percent in '73 while man-hours increased 7.4 percent. All in all, declines in productivity were recorded by 10 industries in 1973 as compared with seven in 1972. The productivity picture then in the steel industry has improved significantly.

It has been increased in the proper manner, it has increased to our mutual benefit. The result is a stronger steel industry more capable of recapturing lost markets and thereby more able to provide steady employement and greater job security for our members. Last, but not least, our country benefits because rising productivity is essential if American products are to remain competitive to those overseas.

I believe our experience in this joint productivity venture emphasizes the point that corporate management should test fully the creativity and resourcefulness of its employees. Management may be pleasantly surprised by the input of workers in improving production through more efficient operations.

The second of the four generalized categories of corporate responsibilities I mentioned was the attitude of corporations towards consumers. This, of course, involves the question of a diversity of useful or attractive products made available to the public at a fair and competitive price and with decent quality, safety, and reasonable honesty in advertising. Corporate directors certainly have a responsibility in this area and they should share it with the management of the corporation.

The third area concerns management attitudes toward local and national governments. In terms of the local community in which they operate, it's been alleged that very often the interest in the problems of the locality is greater when it is a local company operating in its own home town. This determines its sense of responsibility towards charitable organizations in the community, and towards protecting the community from removal of the plant to another community.

Much of this sense of responsibility is lost when American corporations expand over the whole country in such magnitude that most of their enterprises are merely called branch plants, with corporate headquarters in New York or Chicago or somewhere else. Likewise, the interest of the management would be greater on environmental and tax matters if it remained local. But most of these major corporations to which *Fortune* magazine referred are vast in size, operate nationally or internationally, and are losing their sense of corporate responsibility toward local communities in the United States. This should be a matter of urgent concern for corporate directors.

Also in this third area, I would say that if business is dedicated to operating competitively, it should see to it that the anti-trust laws of this nation are strongly enforced and that the directors and their managements do their part to see that competition is a reality rather than something simply spoken about and then ignored.

Let me here interject a few words about corporate responsibility in accepting a fair share of the tax burdens of their localities and of the nation. This fair sharing should apply not only to corporations, but also to taxes owed by individuals. It is no secret that our tax laws are more regressive than progressive and that low- and middle-income families pay more than their fair share. Additionally, in terms of the nation as a whole, it would seem that corporations and other institutions in the United States should be concerned with strengthening our democratic process, with fighting discrimination in any form, with our environment, and the conservation of the resources of this nation. In all of these areas our corporations should manifest genuine concern and be heard on the right side of the public interest.

Some of you may wonder if I am advocating worker representation on the board of directors of corporations. I say no, quite frankly, I am not. Organized labor is generally opposed to worker members on corporate boards as is done in West Germany under a practice that is known as co-determination. In West Germany union officers actually sit on boards of directors. But it is interesting to note that this practice had a political purpose.

In the thirties, when Hitler was in the process of gaining control of Germany, he did so in part by gaining control of Germany's tremendous industrial complex. And after winning control of huge corporations, Hitler built his military machine and arsenal. After the war the trade unions in West Germany determined not to let it happen again, and they decided that the way to prevent it was to go to the system of co-determination.

The purpose was political rather than economic. But it was also to allow union representation on corporate boards to observe what was happening in the corporation and to see to it that control by any political instrumentality would not re-occur. But as a means of protecting workers' interests, we of labor in this country see little value in labor participation on corporate boards. We maintain that workers must deal with management through the process of collective bargaining. And since their positions are adversary when dealing with management over wages and fringe benefits, it is better that labor unions function as separate institutions and not get involved with boards of directors where interests and responsibilities would be unclear.

We are not opposed to the establishment of special committees set up between management and labor unions for special purposes, such as we did in the major basic steel companies on the question of productivity and promotion and use of domestic steel. It is evident that the labor leader who might sit on a corporate board of directors would face great political and personal hazards since the question of allegiance would be raised by the rank and file members of his union. So, you see, we prefer to continue under our existing system of free collective bargaining.

I would also say in this third area of management attitudes toward local and national governments, that corporations should support the improvement of the welfare of their employees not only through collective bargaining, but also in terms of state and federal legislation, which in most cases they show little interest, or routinely have opposed. Here I want to mention a specific piece of legislation that is of great concern to our union and should be of some concern to management.

I refer to the Landrum-Griffin Act, which has been on the books now for 15 years and has proved to be a continuing source of unfair governmental interference with the internal operations of our union and other unions. Our union has a record of election fairness which we doubt could be matched in public elections if such elections were regulated even half as carefully as union elections.

For example, *Business Week* recently noted, and I quote, they said of our union, "The Steelworkers have gained what is probably unfair notoriety in election cases because it is one of the few major unions, and by far the largest, that conduct nationwide elections at local polling places. Out of 100 separate district elections since the passage of Landrum-Griffin, only nine have resulted in complaints to the Labor Department. Though it has held four elections for top officers since then, not one has brought an actionable complaint."

Now, despite our union's outstanding record of union fairness in the holding of elections at all levels of our union, the Labor Department continues to interfere with our way of holding elections and threatens actions unless changes are made in our referendum procedures. To avoid, as much as we could in the future, such interference by government, our union made additional changes in our election rules during our convention this past September. But I am sure that no matter how many changes we make, the Act will continue to be used to create problems for unions.

Now, let me cite one quick example of the kind of harassment I am talking about. For seven years the Labor Department has been attacking our meeting attendance eligibility requirement for local union office. It requires that a candidate for local union office must attend a certain number of his local union meetings so that the candidate be both knowledgeable and interested in union affairs. The Labor Department asserts that the requirement is unreasonable and it's brought nearly two dozen lawsuits against our locals challenging this rule.

Now, no court has agreed that the rule is unreasonable, yet the Department still brings more suits. You might ask why and we have asked why. But, frankly, it ties the union up in the courts, you see, costs the union money, and it keeps it from better servicing its membership. And we think it is time to repeal the Landrum-Griffin Act or at least give it a drastic overhauling. Some in industry share our viewpoint on this legislation, as was indicated last May when the National Commission for Industrial Peace submitted a report to the White House.

The commission is made up of 10 top industry and union leaders and stated that Landrum-Griffin was a hinderance to, and I quote, "responsible labor leadership," and thus to stable collective bargaining. Now, I would hope that more on management's side would share this viewpoint because the best interests of the public and management are subverted by a law that encourages internal turmoil, that continuously is used to harass democratically elected leadership, and that frustrates a union's ability to establish a stabilized relationship.

Now, the fourth area I wanted to touch on concerns the responsibilities of corporations in an international frame of reference. I would emphasize that labor has a most serious concern over the role of American corporations overseas and the degree to which they endanger American jobs, undermine our economy by excessive export of capital, and diminish the capital available in the United States. The interest of the workers of the United States and the people of the United States is not precisely fulfilled when American business enterprise goes multinational and pursues its interests overseas with abandon.

The U.S. government should not be an overseas policeman for American corporations. And we believe that in every action of corporations overseas, the multinationals should be viewed not just in terms of potential profit, but in terms of the needs of the American workers and the needs of all the American people. We simply cannot continue to allow the exportation of our technology, we cannot continue to allow the deterioration of America's industrial muscle. I am proud that the United Steelworkers of America took an early lead in this struggle against the practice of rich multinational companies to move machinery, technology, and jobs round the globe as if the only name of the game was profit. American workers have lost jobs because American companies, which enjoy tax benefits and incentives from Uncle Sam, have moved their plants to countries where wages are just a fraction of those at home.

As noted in a recent article of the *New Yorker* magazine, two American companies have settled in Hong Kong to take advantage of a labor pool in which 60 percent of the adults work a seven day week and which includes 34,000 children aged 14 or younger, half of whom work 10 hours or more a day. Now, this practice does not benefit the American workers whose jobs are gone. They do not benefit the broken communities and ghost towns which often result because jobs are gone. And they rarely bring true benefit to the workers in the countries to which the companies have moved because the wages are so low and the jobs so insecure. It just doesn't make sense, you see, for this country to go on giving the profitable tax incentives to multi-national conglomerates so they can take their jobs and their payrolls away from America. If we continue to export our technology, our capital, and our jobs, we run the risk of winding up as a service nation.

If the free enterprise system as we have known it is to persevere, then the private enterprise sector has to function more and more in behalf of the need of this total society and in a sense transform itself into a newer role of social responsibility. As the chairman of B. F. Goodrich, C. Pendelton Thomas, stated in a recent speech reported in the *Pittsburgh Press:* "It's time for more business people, working through their organizations and acting independently as private citizens, to take a more energetic, active part in political and social causes to preserve and perfect our economic and political systems for the good of all the people."

Now, Mr. Chairman, I will close my remarks with an appeal to the good sense of corporate leadership to set aside the outdated myths that unions are out to destroy free enterprise or that unions are nothing more than a thorn in industry's side, to be tolerated but never fully accepted. I would also call for rethinking of corporate policies that will be more consistent with our changing society and more pragmatic in coping with the realities of today. Labor has supported and functioned within the free enterprise system and it wants to see the free enterprise system preserved, but it cannot save free enterprise if its practitioners are determined to commit suicide.

Question: Please comment on the continued widespread existence of featherbedding in light of your promise of increased productivity.

Mr. Abel: I don't know where the featherbedding is that the questioner refers to. It certainly is not in the steel industry. We have never had that problem and we don't have it now. The only place alleged to have widespread featherbedding was the railroad industry, but I think recent years have disclosed that there was perhaps more of that in the board rooms of the directors and management. (Laughter.)

Question: Mr. Abel, Mr. Casey stated that foreign plants of U.S. companies do not export jobs because: 1) this is the only way U.S. companies can compete, it would not otherwise be able to produce and sell; and 2) on balance more and not fewer jobs are thus created. Would you please comment.

Mr. Abel: Well, No. 1, I know Bill Casey well. We have been good friends for some time. Bill in my judgment hasn't been in too good a position to observe the impact and the effects of the development of multinationals. And I can only say to you that in my observation we have been severely damaged by both the export of jobs through the development of the multinationals as well as the infringement on American markets because we haven't had adequate legislation on our statute books.

In our industry, as an example, in the year 1971 there was imported into this country 18,300,000 tons of steel. Now, that capacity represents 109,000 American steelworker jobs. It was made possible because of the fact that American free enterprise steel industry was required to compete with the socialized steel industry in countries like Great Britain, as an example, that need not make a pound; it makes no difference if they lose 10 pounds. They compete with the Japanese, whose government allocates raw materials on a quota basis through the amount of steel that is exported to the U.S. This is what we consider unfair competitive positions. We asked our government to repeal these or do something about it, and they have done little or nothing. We have been losing jobs in spite of what Bill Casey says.

Question: Has your union become active in social action? Also, have you been successful in creating equal opportunities for women and blacks in your union?

Mr. Abel: Yes, we became a constitutional organization in May of 1942. Our first constitution provided a provision at the outset making membership and supporting workers in jobs irrespective of race, creed, color, national origin. We have maintained an active civil rights department and civil rights committee. We have been supportive of all these kinds of activities. We are presently going through a redoing of our whole seniority procedure. And in any instance where it is alleged that some individual has been deprived of an opportunity because of past practices, adjustments are being made for that.

Question: Has not the Landrum-Griffin Act enabled the federal government to clean up truly corrupt union conditions, for example, the Mineworkers situation?

Mr. Abel: No, I don't credit Landrum-Griffin with that at all. There are a number of things that went into the problems of the Mineworkers, mainly stagnation over the years both of the industry as well as the union itself, and failure of the industry to induce younger and more active workers. It was a general deterioration, I would have to say, and then there developed an internal feud not among younger and older people, but among older people.

Question: What is your union's position regarding EEOC actions that force the management into aggressive affirmative action programs involving quotas and time-tables?

Mr. Abel: Well, I just made reference in answer to the other question along those lines. But to give you a better view of our position, our thinking on it, we joined with our industry, the basic steel industry, and the government in a consent decree and we have implementation committees in every region and in every plant of the steel industry presently in the process with the joint management-union effort to take care of this problem.

Question: Does labor want to see free enterprise preserved in health delivery or does it want government financed and operated health delivery systems?

Mr. Abel: We are in support of the national bill and we are in support of it primarily because of the failure of the industry, so-called, to meet its social responsibilities and to make it possible for all Americans to have proper health care. We do support the national health bill.

Question: What is your view as to the proper framework for political activity by corporate management and stockholders in view of the freedom of labor to collect large sums of money for the purpose and engage in massive organized political activities?

Mr. Abel: Well, I know of no differentiation between the rights of management to collect sums of money, whether they be large or small, any different than that of labor. There is a great misunderstanding with respect to labor's participation. Labor, like the corporations, is not permitted to use trade union monies for political purposes. But labor is permitted to raise on a voluntary basis monies to be used in political purposes, just as corporate leadership is permitted to raise individual contributions and make that available.

So, frankly, there is no difference, and I see no reason for any change myself, although we do favor more government financing of political campaigns because our system is made prohibitive for the average person to seek public office.

Question: You expressed concern about branch plant configuration of corporations and its negative local impact. National unions with many locals have the same problems. How do you suggest corporations act to insure adequate local performance?

Mr. Abel: One of the ways, of course, and I don't know how you do it in the broad corporation sense, maybe 70 or 80 plants in 70 or 80 different locations, but one way is to give more authority to the local management to play a role in community activities; and too often this is not done. The corporate policies, the corporate thinking is on a national basis rather than a community or local basis.

Question: Are you in favor of wage-price controls?

Mr. Abel: No, I prefer that we operate in our free system. We objected several years ago when they were imposed. We said that we wouldn't see equity and we didn't. And we of labor withdrew from it and that brought an end to the feeble attempt several years ago to maintain some kind of control system. At the present time we still maintain our position of opposition. I would say, however, that if we get into an economic posture of perhaps eight percent unemployment rate and still an eight percent inflation rate and the government develops and proposes a system that will provide fairness and equity to all segments of our economy, the labor movement will certainly cooperate and make its sacrifices and its contributions as any other segment of the society.

How to Assure Effective Senior Management

Harold Koontz

University of California, Los Angeles

Dr. Koontz is Mead Johnson Professor of Management, Graduate School of Management, at the University of California, Los Angeles. He is a Director and Consultant to the Farr Company, and a consultant on management and management development to various companies throughout the United States and abroad.

Dr. Koontz has had a diverse experience in business and government. He has been a Director of Commercial Sales, Consolidated Vultee Aircraft Corporation; an Assistant to the President and Director of Planning of TWA; an Assistant to the Vice President in Charge of Research for the Association of American Railroads; a Transportation Consultant to the Office of Price Administration; and a Cost Analyst for the Trustees of the New York, New Haven and Hartford Railroad. In addition, Dr. Koontz has written many books and articles on management, and taught business and economics at several universities.

I believe, and many speakers in this conference have pointed it out, that we in this country have recognized the tremendous importance of management in all types of enterprises. We are in the United States regarded as the leaders in the management movement, a movement which I find has spread rapidly over the world, and, as I even found some 15 years ago in such countries as Japan, where management was regarded virtually as a religion.

As we look at this field of management, we find that in virtually every business, government enterprise or agency; educational, charitable, or other enterprises; by law and by society; by logic; there sits at the top of these enterprises a board or commission charged with the responsibility for managing these enterprises. This means, as we know, to make sure that they are being managed efficiently and effectively. You know well that when a company meets a disaster, as we saw in just the last few years with such companies as Penn Central, Equity Funding, LTV, and others I could name, one of the first cries that goes up from the public and financial analysts is: "Where was the board of directors?" And it is a proper cry.

We know that our boards of directors leave much to be desired. As we look at their role and as we look at the studies made by various people, we find some very disappointing things: confusion as to the role of boards; how do they manage; how much; do they try to do something active or are they passive observers, casual observers?

We find in some boards: weak boards; directors who do not direct; rubber stamps; directors who think of themselves as advisers to the chief executive. Investigators have even found a surprising number of chief executives who wanted their boards to be nothing more than advisers. We find also a lot of the "insider" syndrome. We find, in addition, the business executive syndrome where we pick as outsiders for the board of directors, executives from other large companies of similar status, going to the same clubs, perhaps even of the same religion, usually with the same kind of thinking. This is one of the things that we know has gotten boards into trouble.

We find insiders, chief executive officers, who don't want a strong board. We find very little training in boards of directors. I have myself led seminars for corporate directors in such countries around the world as Australia, England, Belgium, Egypt, South Africa, and others, but this is only the second time I've been asked, or have even heard of a seminar *for* corporate directors. I do believe this conference is a very great occasion, at least so far as the United States is concerned.

We find virtually none of the thorough research and selection techniques for directors that we insist be used for our operating managements. We find boards that leave much to be desired. Yet, no one can deny that there is hardly a greater responsibility of boards than two things: 1) making decisions concerning the long-term success of the company; and 2) making sure the company is well managed.

I have heard many ideas from the public and from my colleagues on this subject. I have heard it said that the board can't really do much about management, that the board's job is to turn this over to the chief executive officer and trust him to make all the decisions and to manage the enterprise well. We do know, as a chief executive is quoted as saying about his board, about boards generally, that "boards do not act until the company has gone to hell." They do not take action until the company is in trouble and there is no ostensible program to get it out. Then and only then they are likely to take action to replace the chief executive officer and perhaps even other members of senior management.

This, of course, as you know, is far too late. To avoid this problem, and I think it can be avoided, and to insure continually that we do have effective management, I do feel that we can do a better job as board members in evaluating and appraising the senior management of the company—senior management which includes, in addition to the chief executive officer, the top vice presidents reporting to him and the division general managers, at least those of important divisions.

We know that appraisal of managers generally is the weakest link in the entire management chain. I have studied appraisal systems in various companies and government agencies in this country and abroad, and I can tell you that I am not at all impressed with the thoroughness, with the accuracy, and with the objectivity with which we appraise managers at all levels. We have made some progress, but still rather too little, despite the fact that appraisal is the Achilles heel in the whole field of management.

The Kind of Appraisal Program We Need

To assure that we, in fact, do have effective senior managers, I propose the same kind of program I would for all managers. It seems to me that to appraise managers, we need to evaluate them on performance in two areas: (1) ability to set and achieve meaningful and verifiable objectives; and (2) ability to manage.

First, appraising managers on their ability to set and accomplish verifiable goals—*verifiable* goals—not fuzzy objectives or goals, such as the virtually meaningless one

I often hear that goes something like this: "It is our objective to make a fair profit while turning out a quality product and being a good citizen in the community."

I would define a verifiable goal as one that, if we set it, we can at some time in the future look back and say, "Yes, we accomplished it," or "No, we didn't." This obviously means that goals in quantitative terms are the easiest to verify, but there are too many objectives that cannot be put in quantitative, measurable terms. I know that one of our prominent companies has put everything in quantities all down the line. Their program of managing by objectives is a farce, simply because people are learning to play the numbers game. Any subordinate can beat any boss in playing the numbers game.

There are many possible verifiable objectives which are qualitative in nature, such as to develop a training program or an advertising program, certain specified characteristics and targets to accomplish by a certain date.

A second basis of appraisal that I would emphasize is appraising managers on their ability to manage. I want a double-barreled approach to appraisal. In other words, I don't want a person in a managerial position to know everything there is about management, but can't perform. Nor, by the same token, do I like to see a performer in a managerial role who can't manage, because I am sure that the quality of managing eventually makes the difference and performers too often perform (or fail to perform) through no ability of their own, but often by luck or fortunate circumstances.

As I speak of this kind of appraisal, I am not speaking of what is often referred to as a performance audit which deals with the total performance of a company and is contemplated to be done once every three to five years. Although some of the elements of a managerial appraisal might also be found in a performance audit, I am speaking of an appraisal—on the two bases mentioned—of senior management, including the CEO. And such an appraisal should be done regularly, at least once each year.

I am not speaking of Justice Goldberg's committee to supervise company operations, or of a committee between the board and senior management. (I am not as concerned as many knowledgeable people are about drawing a hard and fast line between board-level management and operating-level management, even though I am sure we should define these roles to keep people from getting into each other's business.)

But if we are to carry out our primary responsibility as directors, we must have better ways to make sure that the company is well operated. This can be done, I am convinced. I have been a part in going it in two different companies. We can appraise on the basis of setting goals and setting them in a verifiable way. This is obviously a fall-out of present popular systems of managing by objectives.

However, even in acknowledging how popular MBO is, in my judgment not more than about 20 percent of the programs of managing by objectives in this country are operating successfully. I even have some research backing for this position. A certain group of researchers found, in their study of the MBO programs in the *Fortune* 500 industrials, that only 19 percent of the program were operating effectively. They found that only 50 out of those 500 companies had reasonably successful programs of managing by objectives.

On the appraising of managers as managers, I think we need more than just to say that we are going to appraise management capability. We need standards. I did develop for a multinational company, a number of years ago, a program of appraising managers from the top down on the basis of the essential principles on basics of management. In fact, it came out to 73 check-points divided up in the areas of planning, organizing, staffing, directing and leading, and controlling. It wasn't perfect, but it worked.*

As a matter of fact, when the board adopted this program (I was on that board, and had been a consultant to the company) the Chairman of the Board, who was a full-time executive and head of all overseas operations, turned to me and said, "Before we start this program to evaluate top managers, I want you," pointing to me, "to evaluate me." I'd rather give advice than to do a thing like that. He wasn't a bad manager, but he wasn't very good, either. Finally, I couldn't get out of it, and I said, "If you insist, I will, providing that you allow me to call the shots just as roughly as I can," Well, I did. On a possible score of five as being perfect, he came out 2.9, which in the university would be a failing grade.

I didn't want to report that to him but we met at his club for luncheon, I made sure he had a number of martinis so he would be properly softened up, and then we met in a room together and went over this appraisal. To my interest and surprise, he had appraised himself and came out 2.6, so I was saved by that. But he turned to me after several hours we spent going over every one of these checkpoints and said: "You know, I have attended a lot of management seminars; I have read a lot of management books; I have even read your damn book, but," he said, "this is the first time I understood what management was all about." So I think it can be done.

How Can A Board Evaluate Senior Management?

What then must board members do in order to accomplish this? First of all, a board has to be a reality and not, as Myles Mace called it, a myth. It does need careful definition of the decision areas in which it operates, including definition of its obligation to evaluate the chief executive officer and at least to review his evaluation of other members of senior management. In order to do this, of course, we would need a special committee of the board, which I might call the management audit or management appraisal committee, made up naturally of outsiders to do the basic work.

As I mention outsiders, another point I would like to make clear is that the independent look, the outside look, does not arise from the numbers of outsiders. I have seen boards with only two out of about nine outsiders who operated in a very "outside" way. I have seen boards with seven out of nine outsiders where all seven simply were lackeys of the chief executive, and operated in a very "inside" way. In other words, we do not determine "outsidedness" by simply counting people.

However, I am sure that this management audit committee must be composed of outsiders. It is inconceivable to me that a chief executive officer, for example, could objectively evaluate himself. I think he might be attached in an advisory role; in fact, some CEO's would insist upon this. A management audit committee, or a management appraisal committee, I am suggesting, and I believe it sincerely, that this committee is really far more important than the typical audit committee. Most of our boards, as reported yesterday, do have audit committees whose function it is, of course, to maintain contact with the outside accounting audit firm and to make sure as best

*This appraisal program is explained in H. Koontz, *Appraising Managers as Managers* (New York:McGraw-Hill, 1971).

they can that the company is handling accounting in order to meet adequate audit requirements.

But what is more important to a company than management? Accounting is important from the standpoint of taxes and reporting to shareholders and avoiding troubles with the SEC. But management is the only assurance we have that people in charge of any company will be able to see problems coming in time and do something about them. I would much rather as a stockholder, as a vendor, as a customer, or as an employee, have an audit of the quality of management of a company than an accounting audit.

This management audit committee might also be combined with the bonus committee. It is my feeling that we should allocate bonuses in very large part to individual managers on the basis of their individual performance. Indeed, if, as is done so often, we allocate bonuses on the basis of a person's position and salary level, regardless of his individual performance in the year, we are not getting much for it. In fact, I have said many times as a stockholder that a company that does that is not getting much more incentive from their managers through bonus payments than they get by giving away Christmas turkeys.

But if we can make bonus determinations on the basis of individual performance, we can go pretty far in getting meaningful incentive. With respect to the chief executive, we can work out with him, for a year and perhaps five years ahead, his verifiable goals and objectives. In one case where I have assisted in setting such objectives I did it at the insistence of a board of directors who were not too high on their chief executive. The chief executive objected strongly. We did work out the problems and developed his verifiable goals.

I got the idea that he didn't like me at all, but I did hear from a friend that he remarked after this exercise: "This was the first time I have known what the board expected of me."

With respect to the other members of senior management, those reporting to the chief executive, it seems to me that our board, through the management appraisal or audit committee, can make sure that the chief executive has an effective program of appraising the quality of managers. Also, that he reports the results of these, perhaps quarterly, certainly annually, to the board as a whole or if that doesn't seem feasible, to the board's management committee.

In addition, in order to appraise our management, we can schedule a regular review of senior management programs and performance. I like the idea, even in fairly large companies, of scheduling at each board meeting (and this would require more than four board meetings a year, I can assure you), one or two major areas for review at the board and have the appropriate member of senior management appear to make that presentation and to answer questions.

The board of directors is held in great esteem, I find, by managers. People like to appear before the board. This procedure often avoids the danger of receiving all of our information about what goes on in the company through the chief executive officer. There is also pressure on the individual who is being reviewed to think through what it is he's suggesting and doing. This procedure gives us as board members, too, an opportunity to size up the senior management under the chief executive and to answer such questions as this: "Is the chief executive hiring enough quality?" and, "Who might be his possible successor?"

In this, a board must feel free to cross-examine. One of the shocking things to me in certain studies of boards is how few boards feel they can cross-examine the chief executive or any other insider. I know from experience years ago as assistant to the president of an airline, where one of my jobs was to keep the boss prepared so that he could answer questions at a board of directors' meeting, that one outsider on that board who asked discerning questions could keep that president on his toes. I can assure you as assistant to the president I never wanted him to come back from a board meeting embarrassed.

I think also that the management audit committee at this time, on the basis of the reports from the board, can do something in evaluating members of senior management and allocating bonuses. As a matter of fact, I would, as I have indicated, tie these together. I have had experience as chairman of a bonus committee in doing exactly that. And in all those years where we varied bonuses in accordance with performance and made no secret about it, giving every man who was on the bonus list a summary of the board committee's evaluation of his strengths and weaknesses, I have known of only one vice president who felt that he was not completely fairly dealt with. The rest of them, all expressed surprise that their bonus was as high as it was. That ties in to one of the simple facts of life—that good people are more sensitive to their weaknesses than proud of their strengths.

If a board is to do this kind of evaluation, it must be an effective board*, not a bunch of bystanders and casual observers. The board must feel that it can take an important review role in a company. Despite these possibilities, and I realize that many companies may feel that this is the talk of an ivory tower professor, I don't believe it really is, and while I wouldn't expect too many companies to develop the kind of appraisal that I have outlined here, I would like to think that some would.

What Do We Do With Ineffective Senior Management?

What if, however, we find that we have some ineffective senior managers? Then what do we do? If we have a decent program of appraisal, the chances are that the chief executive and certainly other members of senior management, will see their deficiencies, either attempt to do everything they can to correct them, or, as I have known in several cases, to take the initiative themselves to ask for early retirement, to resign, or to look for another position.

As for members of senior management below the CEO, usually it takes only a hint, perhaps by an outside director, that maybe a senior manager is not quite right for his job, and we usually can get a replacement. But so far as the chief executive is concerned, we have another problem. What do we do if we find ourselves in the position of having an ineffective chief executive officer?

I have seen a few cases where chief executives detected their own ineffectiveness and did take steps either to resign, take early retirement, or accept a position as a part-time consultant or even as vice chairman of the board.

Also, in the instance where we have a demonstrably ineffective CEO, and where the outside members have enough knowledge, power, and guts, the CEO can be forced to "resign." But these cases are generally too few, since outsiders are likely

*See Appendix, *Questions To Be Asked Concerning Total Board Effectiveness.*

to be the handpicked friends of the CEO and are likely to accept his excuses and "window-dressing" for his failure.

It is probably more important or more feasible in dealing with the chief executive officer who doesn't fit any of these first two categories to hire a consultant. I am talking about one of two types of consultants.

One type is for a company that is a little sick, but not terminally ill. That is the type of consultant who can get the chief executive's attention, respect, and confidence, who comes in to help reconstruct some of the managerial deficiencies in the company. For a company, however, that is really in trouble, then, of course, we are likely to need the "hatchet" type of consultant.

In working with the more helpful, constructive, patient type of consultant we can do things such as organize around the chief executive, let him keep his title, but build up either an executive vice president or an operating vice president. In one smaller company I know, the board even worked out a system for having the division managers of this company report directly to the board.

I can give you some examples of how we might deal with not disastrously ineffective, but *somewhat* ineffective, chief executive officers. One of these examples was a founder, Chairman and President of a company, $200 million in sales, where one outside director, who represented the financial community, sold the board on the idea that with the company's fast growth it better have an outsider, a consultant, look at the organization structure and see whether it was structured for growth. The result of that study was that chairman and president, who was a great entrepreneur, kept his chief executive officer title and became only chairman. A strong president was brought in, and the company was saved.

In another case, a chief executive, who did happen to be the founder, an admitted genius, accepted an underwriter's recommendation to the board to engage a consultant and have him make a study of managerial strength for growth. The chief executive accepted this recommendation because he believed that the consultant would recommend to him that he fire a certain vice president. A consultant was brought in and this resulted eventually in this particular company appointing one of the vice presidents as executive vice president and removing to some extent the chief executive from operating the company.

In another very large company, the chairman, and chief executive officer, one of the greatest entrepreneurs in our country, really couldn't manage his fast growing company. The company suffered unexpectedly one year a huge loss. The result was that financial analysts and the business press greatly criticized this particular man. To save face he was led to hire a consultant who made some significant recommendations.

First he recommended that they not be in too much of a hurry to appoint a new president, because this chairman had already gone through several presidents. He did have him appoint three executive vice presidents and institute such rather simple changes as having regular review of division managers by the executive committee of the board and have an outside director, in whom the chief executive had a great deal of confidence, participate actively on this executive committee. This largely removed the chief executive from his position as managing head of the company and allowed him to do what he could do best, which was to be an entrepreneur.

I could go on and on. All this is to say that when you are encountering this kind of problem at the CEO level, it is a difficult problem. In the case of a very sick company, one I would call virtually terminally ill, we do need what I call the "hatchet" type of consultant. They are usually brought in to such a company at the insistence of a bank that is afraid it is going to lose its millions of dollars in loans. These are usually companies headed by a chief executive who is incompetent, who is arrogant, and who doesn't want any help. This can call for roughness.

In some companies the board may not be able to move. I know I suffered in a company, a public company, as an outside director with a top management that I knew was driving the company downhill. But our board was divided evenly and we couldn't move. Finally the hatchet type was brought in at the insistence of the bank. After just a few weeks of analysis he came in to the board and said that he would recommend to the bank calling of the loans if we did not replace the chief executive. That carried the day and the chief executive was replaced.

Boards Should Make Departure Painless

When we force any member of senior management from the job, I feel that we have to ask ourselves some questions: was it really his fault; was he carefully and accurately selected; did we on the board give him the support and help and direction that he needed? Often that is as much the board's fault as the executive's fault, or as much the chief executive's fault as it is that of the other members of senior management. In those cases, I feel that it is not only right, but it is practical, that we be quite generous in severance arrangements.

I say that it is practical because I remember cases such as the one in which a president of an airline was unceremoniously kicked out of the airline and ended up shortly after that as head of the Federal Aviation Administration. Where a president of a company was kicked out and ended up as the president of the company's largest customer. Where the president of a university was booted out of the presidency, and turned up as top executive of one of the largest foundations that tend to give money to universities.

So let's be practical about it. And I would hope that when a man does leave a company, when he is forced out, if you will, he can be forced out painlessly and in good humor. I would hope that more executives replaced could be like Clark Kerr was when he was discharged from the University of California. He said, as some of you may remember, "The circumstances on which I entered the presidency and the circumstances upon which I left it were exactly the same. In both instances I was fired with enthusiasm."

Needed: An Effective Board

So as we look at this, I realize that this whole question of how we insure effective senior management or, how we deal with ineffective senior management simply adds up to this: are we sure we have an effective board? Second, are we taking steps to assure that we have effective senior management, rather than waiting for action after disaster strikes?

In my humble opinion, American boards have not been doing what they could in these areas. I realize that this is difficult. I realize that all managing is difficult, demanding, and complex. As a matter of fact, even mathematically there is no more complex a role in our whole society than managing. As I tell my MBA students, it is the most frustrating job that you will ever have and do not go into management unless you can handle the frustration, because people are the most frustrating of all.

Question: In addition to board evaluation of the CEO in order to maintain a high level of effectiveness between the board and the chief executive, can you comment on what methods, if any, you would suggest in having the CEO evaluate the board performance?

Dr. Koontz: I don't think there is any doubt that he can and he should evaluate the board and present his evaluation to it. He knows it well. Now, the standards are not I think, as easy and clear as they are for pure managing, but if he has, with the board's approval, obviously, set up the areas in which board decisions are to be made, a simple chart of approval authorization, then he can very well say to a board, and his chairman really should be doing this, "One of my criticisms of you people is that you don't stick to your business and you try to get into the operating areas."

Question: What is the job of the board in appraising performance of directors as directors and what should they do about a low appraisal of the board?

Dr. Koontz: Well, I have noted suggestions by several people that there should be an officer of the board or an outside consultant should be brought in and observe the board, whose job is to appraise board members and the whole operation of the board. I would think that what I called the management audit committee might be a good one to focus on the operation of the board. And I believe we could learn a great deal if we did get that kind of evaluation.

Question: Do you think there is a conflict between a man being at the same time a director and a consultant to a corporation?

Dr. Koontz: Well, it depends upon, I think, what he is a consultant for. I have worried about that myself on occasions. In most cases I have not been active as a management consultant in a company where I am director. In other cases it has been advantageous for me to do so because I had a long association with the company. But if you are consulting in the basics of management, this is not the same kind of conflict, I think, as if you are consulting on marketing, some technical area, or labor relations, or whatnot.

Question: What should the chief executive officer do about an ineffective or inattentive outside director?

Dr. Koontz: We do need a chairman who is separate from the chief executive officer. Now, if you do have that, the CEO can use the chairman as his representative for the board. I think a good chairman can go far in getting board members to stick to their job. And if a person is just purely inattentive, well, you will have to find some way to get him off the board, although I grant you that is not the easiest thing in the world.

I have served on boards where we had that kind of person. Where a person simply does not come to the board meetings, then I think we have got to take action. I think a person has to attend three-quarters of the board meetings or he shouldn't be on the board.

Question: In view of repeated reference about the General Motors board procedure, is it not significant that CEO's are selected with but few years to serve as president, perhaps emphasizing team management on a continuing basis?

Dr. Koontz: I don't think that that practice in General Motors over-emphasizes team management. In fact, I am very suspicious of that word as most people mean it. It doesn't mean you don't have a team, but remember this, any athletic team worth its salt has people who play given positions for which they are specially trained, follow play patterns in which they are specially trained, and someone calls the signals. Now, in the GM situation it is true that by and large, in recent years especially, the senior management, the chief executive officer, who is usually the chairman, of course, and the chief operating officer, who is the president, do have relatively short tenures of roughly five years.

Many people would argue that that is enough. I remember a very prominent business executive who believed strongly that nobody should serve as chief executive officer for longer than six years. He also had the idea that the CEO would leave his position but serve on the board of directors as a member of a planning committee, continuing to receive his salary. The only weakness of that is, if a man is retired too young from the CEO's position, will he really stay with the company and be satisfied to be a member of a planning committee of the board?

Question: What would be included in your verifiable objectives that you mentioned for the corporation, the verifiable ones, with recent cases like Penn Central and legal suits against board members? Can a board member afford to be uninformed or fail to face up to serious problems of corporate planning and management performance?

Dr. Koontz: As I tried to make clear, I use the term "verifiable" rather than "measurable" because of the danger of overdoing the numbers game. Many of the chief executive's objectives except for sales and profit levels and this sort of thing, such as the introduction of a new pricing system with certain characteristics, will be qualitative.

There is a way, however, and I believe this does tie in objectives. If the CEO has clear, verifiable objectives and he knows what they are and the board makes clear that it is going to evaluate on these, then the board will know what information it needs to know. You will never wait until a year or five years are up before you see whether a man has achieved his objectives, but you will know what you need to know. And the trouble with boards today, as with many managers, is that they don't know what they need to know in order to do their jobs. I have seen the changeover in a few good MBO programs where, with verifiable objectives, every manager involved from the chief executive officer on down, now knew what information he needs to know. Likewise I think the board, too, would know better if it established and enforced clear objectives for senior management.

Creative Tension:
The Board-CEO Relationship

John F. Magee

Arthur D. Little, Inc.

Mr. Magee is President and Chief Executive Officer of Arthur D. Little, Inc. He joined the company as the first full-time member of the Operations Research Group, of which he became head in January 1969. From 1963 to early 1968 he headed the Management Services Division. Mr. Magee has worked with clients on assignments in marketing and advertising research; production planning and inventory control; transportation, communications, and distribution cost analysis; and managerial control. Mr. Magee is the co-author, with David M. Boodman, of Production Planning and Inventory Control, *second edition, published by McGraw-Hill in 1967. He has also written* Physical Distribution Systems *and* Industrial Logistics: Analysis and Management of Physical Supply and Distribution Systems, *and several technical papers and survey articles in the fields of management and management research. He is a member of several boards of directors.*

I would like to describe an example of how one quite active board works and see what conclusions we can draw from this. The example is the board of directors of a moderate-sized resource management company. It is an unusual board and an unusual company. The operating characteristics of this board indicate some of the requirements both on board members and on the chief executive officer in order to get what I will characterize as an active leadership board. I have served on a small number of boards of directors and have participated as a consultant in other board activities when boards have considered issues on which I have worked professionally. I have also read a fair cross-section of literature on boards.

With this background and experience, it is my observation that the conventional off-hand judgment of the proper role of the board of directors—to hire a good chief executive officer and then sit back and judge his performance—is quite widely held in practice, even though it is not necessarily preached. I am not here to analyze that particular point of view because a lot of others have done so more effectively than I could. But I do hope this example that I will discuss will show that the conventional view is not the only way. I will try also to relate the differences in the style of board operations, the conventional style or the active leadership style, to two concepts of how management might work.

In summary, I will describe how one board of directors is organized and operates in order to draw conclusions as to why it works and to relate these to a concept of open management, a concept I think is quite important in the process of formulating policy and strategy.

The company I will talk about is a resource management company with about $350 million in assets under management. These assets include five major operating units or wholly-owned or controlled businesses, participation in a number of major private investments, and a portfolio of marketable securities.

The company was once a subsidiary of a much larger company. Now it has a completely independent board of directors and a completely new and independent management. This means that both board and management are new in their jobs, at the most about four years. So both have had to develop a method of working together and a style of management. To some extent I suppose that's been an advantage, because they haven't been trapped by traditions or caught with personalities that they had to live with.

But, in any case, the objectives the board has set for the company are quite clear and have been quite clearly transmitted to the management: To maximize the growth in the value of the net assets of the company. To that end the board has given the management some strong financial incentives. The board is a group of nine people, of whom three are insiders and six outsiders. The three insiders occupy three key roles in the organization. One is the President and chief executive officer, who also serves as chairman of the board; the other two are senior officers with major responsibility for key operating units of the company. The outsiders include three businessmen, two of whom are chief executive officers in their own companies; two members of the financial community; and one business school professor with a focus of interest in finance and policy.

Actually, even though this board is only about four years old, it has had quite a bit of turnover because of other demands on its members or conflicts of time or interest. So there has been change, but even with that change the style of operation has continued.

The board operates as a whole and through a few committees. The organization committee has four outside members. It is a committee that is concerned with the effectiveness, compensation, incentives, and recruitment of senior management. The audit committee includes all the outside directors and has the normal functions that have been discussed for the modern audit committee. The securities committee is peculiar to this company, I suppose. It is a group who advise senior management on major transactions affecting the marketable securities portfolio.

In addition to committee service, the outside directors also serve as links between the board as a whole and the operating units of the company. For example, an outside director will serve as either a member of the board of each subsidiary company or a member of an executive advisory group of a division; these directors are directly and intimately involved in the operations of the subsidiary business units.

The board as a whole meets on a bi-monthly schedule. Meetings generally run about five hours. The meetings are preceded by substantial advance written briefing material. The weekend before every meeting, a package of briefing material arrives at each outside director's doorstep by courier. The meetings include active participation by advisors such as legal counsel or consultants. And they are active working meetings, not formal exercises to review formal agenda items. In fact, the key committees that I mentioned characteristically meet either the night before a regular meeting or for one or two hours in the morning before. A lot of detailed issues are dealt with in this way and the committee chairman, who is in every case an outside director, can report to the full board and quickly dispose of a lot of material. The committees may also meet fairly frequently between full board meetings.

The organization of the board has something to do with the way it works, the links of outside directors to operating units, the committee structure, and the like, but the principles under which the board operates are particularly important.

One principle is open information flow. I have mentioned the full written briefings. There is a lot of material going to the board members giving them up-to-date information on the current status of operating units individually. There is a flow of information through the individual links between outside board members and the operating units. And there is a lot of informal contact encouraged between the outside directors and members of the senior management. So the board is very well informed, and the information outside directors receive is not sterilized information. Full flow of information is encouraged.

A second key principle of the board operation is that debate in the board is very actively solicited. This takes some hard work, I believe. For one thing, open issues are brought to the board. I think one way that active debate is encouraged is that issues are brought to the board and discussed at the begining of the period when management is starting to work on them, when they have to do with major questions of strategy or resource allocation. Issues do not first come to the board in the form of set proposals for board ratification. I have mentioned the participation of advisors; the advisors are there to speak their minds and to give the board a feeling for the full nature of the problems and the alternatives. The board thus has an opportunity to make input, to help structure the issue, and to develop the issues as the work goes along.

So the board operates with an open flow of information, active encouragement of debate, and between meetings a lot of informal contact to review positions and understandings. Then, like any good board, it finally takes formal action. This set of principles has some important effects.

I have mentioned that the directors know what is going on. They feel that, and they appreciate it; they recognize the responsibility to use information responsibly within the organization. The process of bringing issues before they are closed, before the solutions are all packaged and wrapped with management's seal of approval, the practice of bringing the unformed issues to the board for preliminary debate, helps make maximum use of the brains that are on the board. The outside directors really do have a chance to shape major moves that the management is considering. As a result, the outside directors have a real sense of contribution. One product of that sense of contribution is that they work very hard.

I want now to digress into a bit of management philosophy. I think that most of us all tend to feel comfortable with what can be characterized as the "line management" approach. This concept of management assumes that information flows in from the field or from operations, and moves up through the system, and decisions move down; that top level management makes the big decisions and the lower levels carry these out, making what subordinate decisions may be necessary.

Good management, according to this concept, implies a clear definition of responsibility at various levels, clear channels of communication, and generally only one channel of communication, so that the signals are unambiguous. It also implies firm decision making, with strategy formed at the top and tactical decisions made further down in the organization. This approach, I think, works fine where the strategy has been determined, where the objectives are clear, and where the problem is one of executing a program. It is this style of management that I think led the, among other things, American Institute of Management some time ago to give the Vatican such high marks—the characteristic of what we'd expect in a good military organization in the midst of a major campaign. It is probably characteristic of the style we could expect of a good consumer products company that knows its product areas, is working in well-established markets, in a secure established economic and social environment (if those exist any more).

But the line "management" approach gets into difficulty when you get into questions of goals and strategy, because what is supposed to be "information-up" turns out to be "proposed answers-up." The options for alternative resource allocation or alternative strategies get screened out at lower levels, including the level of the chief executive officer, if these options are seen to be inconsistent with lower level priorities or lower level perceptions. This creates at the board level a real dilemma. The outside director can either dig for information and alternatives, and as a result appear to attack or challange management, and create a lot of destructive tension by this process; or you can sit back and ratify the management proposals that are brought to you all packaged up.

I think there is another point of view or possible style of management. I have characterized this for the purposes of discussion today as the "judicial-political" approach. I am not very proud of that particular title; some people have called it the adversary approach or the advocacy approach.

Under this concept of management of an institution, information and knowledge are assumed to be developed at *all* levels. Basic issues can be formulated at any level and move up through a process of advocacy and debate and resolution. Our judicial system works that way. Some of the most fundamental issues concerning the values of our society are raised in the context of very specific cases in the police courts of our major cities. These move up through the system through a process of adversary debate or advocacy until they may finally be resolved at the level of the Supreme Court, still in the context in which they first arose, but for the purpose of establishing some fundamental questions of value or social goals.

This concept of managing a system relies very heavily on open advocacy and debate, to bring out facts, to air assumptions, and to test issues of values. Both management systems, I suggest, are actually at work in most organizations, most if not all the time. The well-organized "line management" style is useful when key choices have been made and are well understood through the organization, and the time has come to implement the program. This style or point of view toward good management has an operating focus.

The open "judicial-political" or advocacy approach is most appropriate when the issues to be dealt with are strategy, objectives and the use of resources. This is real board-level material.

A lot of us are uncomfortable or impatient with the process of open debate or advocacy. We like to avoid it. We think that decisions should be made by executives on the basis of rational analysis. We don't like the idea of "playing politics." We don't like to get into arguments or debates. Sometimes we may even associate disagreement over issues with personal dislike or attribute disagreement to improper self-serving motivation.

Well, in the advocacy approach to management you assume that certain positions are going to be self-serving. Of course they are. But you recognize that and you force the alternatives into the open for consideration. I think it is important in business to recognize that this adversary or advocacy process is going on all the time when we address questions of resource allocation or strategy, questions where there are bound to be differences in perception and values and differences in conclusions. I think it is important to recognize that advocacy is going on and to use it effectively. The thrust of my argument today is that the board is one place where this process really is needed and where a company, to have an effective, creative board, needs to nurture this process.

What does it take? I'd say the chairman is key. It takes a chairman who understands and is comfortable with advocacy and debate, a chairman who is conscious of both the substance and the process; that is, one who is well aware not only of what is being said, but what is happening between the people. It takes a chairman who can put up with ambiguity, because this process is not quite as tidy as the other approach, where the neatly wrapped package comes in and comes back out still neatly wrapped with the label of approval.

The results of this process may not come out quite as expected and it may take more time to resolve questions, because the chairman must not only allow points of view to be expressed, but also see that the issues are fully developed. That in turn means that there needs to be a lot of attention to the agenda of meetings. With all due respect to some of my friends who are secretaries of boards, I think sometimes secretaries of boards like to get the agenda organized so that the ''necessary'' items, the less important housekeeping items, are put up front and can occupy all the available time so the board can avoid getting to the important but more controversial ones.

A second key requirement for this process to work is that indeed there be free access to facts and not a process that feeds the board sterilized management-serving information. There has to be, through that process, an opportunity to develop real alternatives, really to look at the pros and cons, really to get independent points of view on those alternatives, and to examine the assumptions that underlie them. A lot of alternatives can look good. The key issue is what set of assumptions you are going to live with.

Finally, I think it takes a group of board members who understand the rules of the process of advocacy. First of all, homework is necessary. You can't debate from ignorance. Secondly, though, a lack of technical understanding is no excuse for not asking for clarification. You have to be prepared to look dumb from time to time. Third, disagreements have to be focused on substance and not on people. Finally, once a decision is made, the opponents in the debate must come together, and give the chief executive officer the support he needs to execute the decision.

I have been impressed by how effectively members of our judicial and political systems and other systems, where advocacy and adversary processes work, are able to do this. I think such skill is needed at the board level because the issues that we are talking about, that the board should be talking about, need real open debate. I think that with a board and a chairman that will support and work with a real advocacy and debate process you can achieve creative support that will go beyond sterile backstopping of the chief executive.

Question: John, could you clarify a little bit here? Do you imply here that the separation of the CEO from the board chairman is an essential part of this process?

Mr. Magee: I didn't mean to. In this case the chairman is the chief executive officer. I think there are things *pro* and *con* to be said about that separation. The choice is not essential to the process that I was describing.

Question: Has the company you described had any problem of the CEO not taking leadership or, alternately, some of the outside directors getting involved in conflicts due to their involvement at the operating level? First question, part of this, has there been any problem of the CEO, with all of this advocacy and whatnot, really not taking hold, which is normal in a line organization?

Mr. Magee: No, I think he is a very strong person who once he makes up his mind, from the debate going on, is very good at coming to a resolution and articulating what he wants to do. Now, because issues are debated over a period of time, as he is working out his thinking and as the organization is working through its studies, the board is brought along. In the end, you can't say that the board told the chief executive what to do or the chief executive told the board. It is a process of contemporaneous and mutual education.

Question: How about the other part, John, where the conflict of interest gets involved with operations?

Mr. Magee: Well, I know people can be concerned whether, for example, having the outside directors actively involved with the individual operating units could create a problem. There is a potential for a problem there, but effective use of directors in this way depends on the outside directors recognizing that they individually are there in order to learn and to give advice, but not take executive responsibility. They have, therefore, to act with some discretion. So far they have been able to do that very effectively. I think that the "problems" of outside directors having involvement with and thus access to lower level operating information can be way overblown.

Question: Why not use different styles in the same company on different issues: A) where the CEO has a definitive answer or B) where the decision to be made is very complex and the ideal solution is not clear?

Mr. Magee: I think that is fair and it is a good idea. The point I want to make is that you do need to open up the style where the issues are complicated. Many basic issues concerning resource allocation are complex; you need to open up the style and you need a management that doesn't feel that somehow its prerogatives have been threatened or it is subject to criticism if it comes to the board with an open question rather than a tidy package.

Question: Is there some norm or concept as to the minimum number of board meetings public corporations should hold during the year?

Mr. Magee: I don't know of any norm, but I would say this. I think if you have a full board meeting only three or four times a year, then it would be pretty hard for the board to have the time really to dig into some of the key issues. Furthermore, it would be pretty hard for the board members as a whole to have the kind of opportunity to participate in the development of alternatives over the course of time.

In such situations, especially if the board is very large, it may be that this process has to be focused on an executive committee. But we have found that the process of meeting about once every couple of months with the opportunity for informal contact to be pretty good. We were meeting once a month for a while and we discovered that we were spinning our wheels.

Question: Does not this system cause the board to become part of operations and, therefore, is it difficult to do an adequate job of judging the CEO?

Mr. Magee: Well, it depends on what you see the board's responsibility to be. The issue depends upon the effectiveness with which you decide what issues the board is going to work on. We see it as a board-level responsibility to be concerned with objectives, with basic strategy, and with basic or major resource allocation questions. We expect the CEO to provide leadership to the board in exercising these responsibilities but not to take some responsibility for them. We don't see the board getting into debates concerning specific operating matters, operating units, or administrative matters at corporate headquarters level.

What the SEC Expects
of Corporate Directors

Ray Garrett, Jr.
Securities and Exchange Commission

Ray Garrett, Jr. is Chairman of the Securities and Exchange Commission. From 1958 until joining the commission he was a partner in the Chicago law firm of Gardner, Carton, Douglas, Children and Waud. From 1954 to 1958, he was on the staff of the Securities and Exchange Commission, and prior to that served as a teaching fellow at Harvard Law School, an Assistant Professor of Law at New York University, and, for several years, a visiting lecturer at the Northwestern University School of Law.

In 1965, Mr. Garrett was Chairman of the Section of Corporation, Banking and Business Law of the American Bar Association, and he has served as Chairman of the Advisory Committee for the Corporate Debt Financing Project of the American Bar Foundation.

In a major address during his term of office, my immediate predecessor spoke of the Commission's concern for the uncertainties which had descended upon the directors of business corporations, in part because of actions and utterances of the Commission. He thought it only fair that directors, present and prospective, have available a reasonably clear idea of what conduct is required to avoid personal liability under the federal securities laws and to avoid suffering civil actions for injunction on our part and the sometimes painful collateral consequences of such actions.

To this end he stated that the Commission would prepare and publish a set of guidelines on the duties of directors. I think this is an appropriate time to announce that we have abandoned the project; an announcement that probably does not come as a surprise to those who have had a particular interest in the idea and had been waiting in vain for something to appear, but an announcement also that obviously comes as a relief to some of you and to some very nervous corporate lawyers that have told me, "For God sake, don't put out anything tentative and then try to back off from it."

We have not made this decision because of any lack of concern for the desirability of directors, like all citizens, knowing or at least having the means of knowing what the law expects of them. We have simply concluded that we cannot effectively advance the cause through guidelines. To the extent there is genuine uncertainty in the minds of thoughtful persons, we may use other means, including speeches such as this, to enable businessmen and their counsel to know at least the state of our thinking.

I have already been subjected to the unfriendly observation that the law must be so confused that we cannot set it down clearly and yet we stand ready to attack any director when, after the fact, we think he has offended against some unknown rule or standard that we conjure up for the purpose. This, we are told, leaves the director at helpless hazard while we remain free to pounce whenever we feel like it. My announcement today will surely intensify such criticism, except to the extent that I can refute it in the remainder of my remarks, which I shall try to do.

Before getting into the substance of our laws, let me say a few things about the process in the law, because the now aborted guidelines project brings a basic and persistent problem of method into sharp focus. In the limited area of our jurisdiction, we are faced frequently with a fundamental choice facing government in general. In a broad sense it is the choice between the common law and the civil code. When should the law be developed through legislation and when should it be through litigation, that is case by case, through judicial or administrative decisions? If there is legislation, should it set forth only general standards, leaving specific applications up to the courts, or should it be detailed and precise?

Congress has taken both approaches in our statutes. Contrast the broad language relating to material false statements and omissions with the specificity in Section 16 (b) of the Exchange Act relating to profits from short-swing trades. Suppose we suspect a director or other insider of having sold shares while possessed of adverse undisclosed information about the company. In deciding whether to act on such a case, we must decide whether we think we can establish that the information was material; that he knew it or should have known the information; that the information was not available to the public; and that no reasonable effort had been made to make it available to the public.

The most contentious of these usually is the question of materiality. Now, in lawyer's parlance there is a lot of law on the question of materiality, just as there is on the question of negligence. It is well settled that some types of information, such as the passed dividend where there has been a history of regularity, are indisputably material. But there are some new types of information that do not fit into categories established by precedent.

There is no exhaustive list that, in a close case, the insider could check in a mechanical way and be certain of the answer. After reviewing the many efforts of judges to define the word "material," the draftsmen of the American Law Institute's proposed Federal Securities Code have so far settled on the following: "A fact is material if a reasonable person would attach importance to it in determining his course of action." That is a fair statement, I think, of the law today, although you will find it phrased in many different ways. The insider making the sale must rely on his own judgment or that of his counsel. If the case is at all close on materiality, he is taking a chance. If he does not want to take a chance, he must forego the sale until the news is out.

In contrast, suppose the question is not whether the sale was based on material non-public information, but whether it was made within six months of a purchase and at a profit. Here, at least when the transactions are simple market purchases and sales and the person was a director throughout the period, we have clarity and certainty in the law to about the greatest degree it can be found.

On my assumptions, the only questions would be whether the sale was within 180 days of the purchase and perhaps how much was the profit. Whether there was any material non-public information and, if there was, whether the director knew it, or even whether the person on the other side of the trade knew it, are wholly irrelevant. If the sale followed the purchase by 180 days, the director is liable for his profit.

If it was 181 days, he is not. I have seen men lose tidy fortunes in tragic circumstances because of miscalculations under the clear, simple, and highly predictable provisions of Section 16 (b).

It is a commonly expressed desire of businessmen to have clarity and predictability in the law. Reflection will reveal that you could have too much and the cost from the irrationality and arbitrariness necessarily involved in specificity and precision of rules may be too high.

The cost of clarity in specific instances may also be too high from the point of view of the law enforcer. No one doubts the wisdom of Justice Frankfurter's oft-quoted observation that sometimes it is not so important whether the law be settled right as it is that it be settled. This attitude properly dominates much of commercial law where there isn't any clearly right rule, but it is important that there be a rule that all could know and abide by. Or, to take a simple analogy, there is no element of morality or justice involved in deciding whether we should drive on the left or right side of the road, but it must be clearly settled which one it is.

Compare that to negligence. It is important that people do not drive negligently. If you do drive negligently and hurt someone or his property, you are liable for the damage. A sufficient degree of negligence becomes a crime whether or not you violated any specific rule of the road. How does someone know whether or not he is driving negligently? He cannot know with mechanical exactitude.

The law requires that a driver abide by the rules of the road, drive on the right, obey speed limits, obey various traffic signs; but the driver's duty is not exhausted by obeying the rules of the road. He must also drive with reasonable care, that is to say, not negligently. What is reasonable care? Ultimately it is what the trier of fact, judge or jury, decides conforms to the behavior of a reasonable man under the circumstances. Is this hopelessly vague? There have been thousands of reported cases on this particular problem and the reasonable man standard has proved workable, though much less than precise.

The reasonable man as driver should be awake and sober and driving in a reasonable way for the conditions in which he finds himself. In fairness, does he need and should he have a mechanistic checklist that tells him on a stormy night with wet leaves on the road he may drive at 35 miles an hour, but not 36? Or that at any specific moment he should have on his high lights rather than his driving lights? Such precision would obviously be ridiculous. While we want drivers to stay within prescribed speed limits, drive on the right, and obey other traffic signs, we are certainly not ready to agree that having obeyed these rules, they are free to drive unreasonably for local conditions and harm someone else with impunity.

So it is with corporate directors. Indeed, the business corporation acts of our several states are singularly devoid of helpful guidelines as to good directors' affirmative duties. Most merely provide that the business affairs of the corporation shall be managed by a board of directors. Some go further and set forth the standard of care and standard of conduct, such as that in the performance of their duties directors shall act like a prudent man in the conduct of his own affairs, or like a prudent man who is a corporate director, or a reasonable man who is a corporate director, a version recently adopted in New Jersey. The largest number of cases under state law, however, relate to conflicts of interest and self-dealing. With respect to the affirmative duties of directors, other than just avoiding conflicts and self-dealing, there is not much.

There are certain specific things that the law seems to require, but the ultimate standard has much in common with the legal concept of negligence. Obviously, directors should comply with the state and federal laws directed toward their activities to the extent that there are any. Beyond that, they should attend meetings with reasonable regularity and pay attention to what is going on. But thinking of our travails over the possible guidelines, even on those simple matters what could we do?

I certainly would not favor a guideline that said all directors must attend all board meetings. This might be highly impractical and unnecessary. On the other hand, I would not favor a guideline that says a director must attend at least two-thirds of the meetings if the effect was to exonerate him from attending a particular meeting at which an obviously important matter was considered. This suggests a standard that says the reasonable director shall attend meetings whenever feasible and that if it is not feasible for him to attend most meetings, then he probably should not be a director. Furthermore, when a matter of special importance to a company and its shareholders is to be considered, he should make a special effort to attend and participate.

What guidance can be given to you beyond this? Let me consider some of the substantive problems that arise under the federal securities laws. The most obvious and the easiest to discuss is the burden placed upon directors individually by Section 11 of the Securities Acts of 1933. That act, chronologically the first of our federal securities laws, deals primarily with the public offering of securities by companies. One of its purposes is to clarify, indeed overcome, the then common law attitudes as to who should be responsible for providing full and fair disclosure to prospective investors and bear the consequences of deficient disclosures.

In furtherance of this policy objective, the Securities Act in Section 11 expressly provides for personal liability on the part of individual directors with respect to the contents of registration statements, including prospectuses relating to public offerings. Omitting some details, this section provides that a director of a corporation is liable to a purchaser of the registered securities in money damages for a materially false or misleading registration statement unless he can establish that, after reasonable investigation, he had reasonable ground to believe and did believe that the allegedly deficient statements made in the registration statement were true and not misleading, the so-called due diligence defense.

Section 11 further provides that a director's maximum liability in such a case shall be no greater than the price at which the registered securities were offered to the public. Thus, the section appears to give corporate directors a fairly clear and specific warning as to the possibility and scope of the civil liability they may face in connection with the registered offering of securities to the public by the corporation on whose board they serve, at least under this one section of the Securities Act.

But while Section 11 puts directors on notice of the possibility of liability and defines the extent of the damages they may be required to pay, it contains no precise guidelines defining exactly what directors must do to be duly diligent and thus to avoid liability. Instead of guidelines, the section lays down a standard, namely that in determining what constitutes reasonable investigation and reasonable grounds for belief (that is what constitutes due diligence) is the standard of reasonableness shall be that required of a prudent man in the management of his own property.

That is all the help a director gets from the statute. Beyond this, he must look to his own judgment and that of his counsel, who must look to the few decided cases on the subject, plus his own judgment and experience. It takes judgment to apply the lessons to be gained from decided cases.

The decision that most thoroughly explored the world of due diligence was that of the late Judge McLean in *Escott* v. *BarChris Construction Co.,* decided nearly seven years ago. After finding the registration statement for the BarChris debentures materially false and misleading within the meaning of Section 11, the judge proceeded to examine in great detail the behavior of the BarChris directors as well as that of the other defendants to decide whether they had met the statutory standard of due diligence. One of the deficiencies in the prospectus was the statement of the company's backlog of orders.

The backlog was materially overstated, in Judge McLean's opinion, because, among other things, the construction contracts involved had cancellation provisions which made them much less firm, if not illusory, and these provisions were not disclosed. The directors did not know this. They had relied on the officers and professionals who prepared the statement. That was not enough for Judge McLean. They should have personally read the contracts.

Now, does one derive from this a rule that in all cases in order to meet the standards of Section 11 all directors must read all contracts reflected in a reported backlog of orders, or all contracts reflected in the financial statements at all? In *BarChris*, only a few contracts were involved. The company was obviously in deep trouble and the backlog was of critical importance. While the court did not qualify its comments on this particular aspect by reference to the peculiar circumstances of BarChris, could the same rule possibly apply to a director of a large multinational corporation? Requiring something impossible of a director by way of due diligence deprives him of his defense and makes him a guarantor. So I would conclude that where it is manifestly impossible for a director to read all of the contracts, due diligence does not require him to do so.

Would it help to have a guideline to that effect? I doubt it, because it really wouldn't advance the cause of clarity very far to say that a director need not read all of the contracts when it is impossible is not necessarily to say that he need not read any, especially if one is of salient significance. Or suppose, as must often be the case, it is not literally impossible to read all the contracts, but even to a most conscientious man it seems quite unreasonable and gross waste of time. Or suppose the defense is, "I read the contract, but I did not catch the point which has caused the trouble because it was written in legal prose too turgid for me to penetrate." How much meaning does an otherwise able businessman get from reading a typical 150-page trust indenture?

The answers to these questions must be found in reasonableness under the circumstances and cannot be found in guidelines because we would end up saying the same thing over and over and so hedged that it all comes back to reasonableness. The greatest contribution of *BarChris,* after all, has not been to lay out exact rules of director behavior, but to remind directors that the Congress in Section 11 intended to cause directors, that is to scare them, to do all they reasonably could to insure accurate and complete prospectuses and they can and must do more than simply sign the registration statement, but how much more and what they must do must vary with the circumstances.

Directors' liability for registered public offerings, however, is not the focus of concern of those who are concerned about what the SEC expects of corporate directors. This concern is doubtless directed toward our challenging the directors' involvement in other corporate activities and based upon other statutory provisions and rules. Here the situation is more complicated.

First of all, the Commission has no direct comprehensive jurisdiction over the duties of directors in managing the corporation. Except under Section 36 of the Investment Company Act of 1940, which permits us to sue to remove directors of investment companies for breach of fiduciary duty involving personal misconduct, we must proceed generally on a disclosure theory. That is to say, the director's misconduct may not, in itself, have constituted a violation of the federal securities laws, but it resulted in false or misleading filings with the Commission for false or misleading information being disseminated to investors. While misconduct frequently leads to misinformation, where it does not there might not be a cause of action under our laws. Parenthetically, by ourselves, I mean the SEC's federal securities laws, leaving out state or any other applicable laws, I hope you will not be misled by my oversimplification. The reach of what we at the Commission collectively refer to as the fraud provisions is not limited to false or misleading statements.

Rule 10b-5, the rule on which the type of actions which I am now discussing is most likely to be based, in addition to untrue statements and omissions, also makes unlawful any device, scheme or artifice to defraud; and any act, practice, or course of business which operates as a fraud or a deceit. And one of the interesting questions that gets debated from time to time is whether or not you can have such a thing as a fully disclosed fraud. That is to say, is there anything so bad even though you have explained it all very clearly, is it nevertheless unlawful under this kind of law? We are struggling with that right now in a particular area.

The Exchange Act also outlaws manipulative devices or contrivances which are not founded on disclosures, and I am talking about all of these violations. But I lack a handy word for them all. Internally, as I say, it is customary to lump all these together as fraud. More and more, however, I encounter people who tell me how nervous and depressed it makes them to hear Commission personnel always talking about fraud. So I am trying to avoid that dread word.

But our point of entry, so to speak, with regard to the conduct of directors of publicly held companies in their capacity as directors and not as principals for their own account is normally the commission by the company of a violation of Rule 10b-5 or one of the statutory provisions relating to market manipulation and false filings. If this is true, how do we get to the directors individually? If the company has included misleading financial statements in its annual report, for example, when and how do we proceed against the directors?

First, the how. Except where a public offering is involved and a stop order proceeding is available, and except for removal actions involving investment companies, the procedure normally available to us is a civil action to enjoin further violations of our laws plus, where appropriate, what lawyers call ancillary relief, disgorgement of unjust gains, the appointment of a receiver, or other measures. Our injunctive actions frequently end in consent decrees arrived at in settlement negotiations, and these may involve changes in the board personnel subject to court and Commission approval, the retaining of special counsel for the company to seek out and enforce any claims the company may have for past misconduct, or any other device that seems to fit the situation. Where we think there has been a willful violation of the laws that warrants more severe measures, we refer the case to the Department of Justice for possible criminal prosecution.

That, in brief, is how we proceed. But when do we seek injunctions and other relief from directors individually rather than just against the company and possibly its officers and professional advisors? The truth is that we have not done it very often, but we have done it and we have talked about it and we may well do it again, so the question has current meaning and interest, remembering always that I am now concerned only with the director whose sole involvement is in that capacity. Many directors have other involvements that are the cause of difficulty. We have for years moved against promoters, officers, major shareholders who also happen to be directors, but that's another matter.

In exploring the question, let me begin with the easy case. The directors at a meeting approve the filing of an annual report on form 10–K clearly knowing that in some respect it is incomplete or false and misleading. We have no trouble asserting that in such a case the directors are individually responsible. They made or caused to be made a materially false statement filed with the Commission which is a violation of Section 18 of the Exchange Act. We might assert that they are controlling persons and thus liable for violations of the controlled person, the company, under Section 20 of the Exchange Act. Or we may assert that they aided and abetted the commission of a violation.

I doubt that anyone would have much trouble with such a case. The defendants would no doubt argue about what they actually knew and about the materiality of the deficiency, but if in fact they knew and it was material, the case is easy. The difficult cases are those where the most that we can show is that the defendants should have known or in the exercise of reasonable care in the performance of their duties would have known. These are the tough cases, plus the disagreements about materiality. These are the tough cases not only from the standpoint of proof, but also because they bring me back to where I began. What duty to know can reasonably be imposed on corporate directors?

We tend to think that the duty of care of directors is what most courts have imposed where the question has been put under state or corporate law, whether phrased in terms of the prudent man in the conduct of his affairs or a reasonable man as a director. The difficulty is that few cases have been brought which did not involve either conflict of interest of self-dealing or the business judgment rule, so that practices have become careless and the idea has been lost that directors of publicly-held companies have a prudent or reasonable man duty to investors to provide full and accurate information and otherwise to cause the company to comply with the federal securities laws.

What is new is that we propose to encourage the performance of that duty by appropriate actions. It means adequate attention to the affairs of the company. It means adequate examination into the materials which directors are asked to approve and authorize, and the relevant corporate procedures. Most of all, it means remembering that a director's duty is to investors and not to the individuals who make up management from time to time. It is our experience that the last of these most needs to be kept in mind.

As I have explained, we have no authority or responsibility to enforce directors' obligations directly. We cannot sue a director simply for non-performance of his duty. But in the effort to enforce our laws, we do intend to hold directors responsible for corporate violations, not absolutely responsible as guarantors, but responsible within the standard of performance of their duty imposed upon them by corporate law. Directors are, therefore, obviously responsible for knowingly authorizing or permitting violations to occur and they may be responsible for permitting them to occur unknowingly unless it appears that they exercised reasonable diligence in the performance of their duties and were, nevertheless, unaware of the misconduct or omission.

I would be remiss, however, in creating the impression that reducing the analysis to the simple proposition that directors must use reasonable diligence in causing the company to comply with the federal securities laws as well as other laws, that this provides easy answers for concrete cases. It obviously does not. We are well aware of the trend to demand more of the reasonable director and the growing quandries arising from the different statuses of directors. Is more expected of the inside than of the outside director? I assume yes, but how much more or, the more cogent question, how much less for the outside director, is hard even to phrase much less measure.

Is more expected of the outside director with relevant professional expertise than without it? Again, I think the law is coming to say yes to some immeasurable degree. At least it is saying that the reasonable director must use such knowledge, experience, and expertness as he possesses in considering company matters. But is a director held to a lesser standard if he has special ignorance rather than special expertise? This will become a bigger question to the degree that companies have special interest directors who are not generally experienced in relevant business and financial matters. I am not sure I wish to predict how such persons will be judged.

A recent case, curiously also arising out of the problems of the BarChris Construction Co., presents clearly the sharply differing views on the duties of an outside director to take affirmative steps to find out what company officers are up to and to take measures to prevent illegal activity. In *Lanza* v. *Drexel*, BarChris, while it was still alive, solvent more or less, offered to exchange its stock with shareholders of the Victor Billiard Company. The Lanza family exchanged 20,000 Victor shares, believing BarChris to be a viable solidly-run company, an impression of BarChris's status they received by virtue of untrue statements of various inside directors and officers who made the misrepresentation.

No one questioned the liability of these inside directors and officers who made the misrepresentations. The real issue in the case concerned the liability, if any, of Bertram D. Coleman, an outside director of BarChris, and the partner of an investment banking firm. Mr. Coleman apparently knew, and I must say the case got so far over so many years, I presume, because Mr. Coleman was the only solvent defendant you could still catch, which is so often the case. Mr. Coleman apparently knew that BarChris's financial condition was faltering, but he did not take part in negotiating the exchange offer, did not see or actually know of any misstatements that may have been made to the Lanzas or others, and did not interject himself into the details of the exchange offer.

The plaintiffs alleged that Coleman's knowledge of the likely adverse nature of BarChris's financial condition imposed a duty upon Coleman to advise the plaintiffs or to see to it that they were advised of the adverse information Coleman knew or suspected. The Court of Appeals of the Second Circuit in New York City concluded that a director like Coleman, in his capacity as a director—that is, a non-participant in the transaction—owed no duty to insure that all material adverse information is conveyed to prospective purchasers of the stock of the corporation on whose board he sits.

The dissent took strong issue with the majority and concluded, as this Commission had urged in an *amicus curiae* brief, that Mr. Coleman's special financial sophistication, coupled with his awareness of the increasing misfortunes of BarChris, should have made him vigilant enough at least to inquire whether the shareholders obtaining BarChris stock were fully informed.

While the special capacities of an outside director thus were not held to be determinative of such a director's liability, corporate directors should not take too much comfort from this decision. For one thing, the Commission's position and that of almost half the Court of Appeals for the Second Circuit, is clearly to rely on any special expertise an outside director may bring to the board in determining whether a director has the duty of inquiring and has breached that duty. More importantly, the majority did not purport to answer the same question as the minority and the Commission. The majority opinion simply held that an outside director has no duty to insure that all material adverse information is conveyed to prospective purchasers of the stock of the corporation on whose board he serves. Thus, the majority reached a question that neither the plaintiffs nor the Commission had raised, arguing only that he had a duty to make reasonable inquiry as to whether the full information be conveyed.

In summary, the SEC expects every corporate director to do his duty, but we are not willing to try to tell him what exactly his duty is in every situation in which he finds himself. We are, however, willing to say, indeed eager to say, that we expect directors to take seriously what the law has in fact long required of them; realizing that their duty and loyalty run to investors and not to CEO's, they must overcome the traditional and very human tendency to be compliant good guys and make the job of management more pleasant, and instead take reasonable measures to protect the interests of investors.

We believe that a sincere and diligent effort to perform this duty is sorely needed to preserve confidence in business corporate enterprise and, if accomplished, will keep directors free from personal hazard.

Question: What is your Commission's attitude with respect to the special counsel for outside directors and audit committees and so on?

Mr. Garrett: My predecessor, Bill Casey, formally endorsed the idea of an audit committee. Certainly it is none of our business to lay down rules, we can't lay down rules that every board must have an audit committee. We think it is a very good idea and find it more and more prevalent. Beyond that, we haven't gone for across-the-board healthy companies that are out of trouble, but are negotiating the settlement with companies that are in trouble under our laws; we have negotiated for and gotten special counsel appointed.

But that is not made just to advise the independent directors, it's been actually the special prosecutor in prosecuting corporate claims. We are quite interested in the various experiments that have been going on, like Texas Instruments' policy which you heard about yesterday. I suppose it is worth observing, that you can't really solve this problem by tables of organization, and that any method that is set up can become useless and meaningless if no one tries to make it work diligently, which might also suggest switching around and trying different things in different periods in order to keep people on their toes and diligent.

Question: Much is being read and heard these days about companies buying up their own shares and in some cases going private. Recently Commissioner Summer made a sharp criticism of such action on the part of companies re-acquiring their stock, implying inequitable conduct on the part of Welles, Rich and indicating that the SEC is contemplating regulation of such re-acquisition tactics. However, since then a judge of the federal court has refused to enjoin that corporation, stating that the federal securities law has not made profit-making or shrewd business unlawful so long as a free and fair disclosure has been made. Can you tell us what the likely position of the SEC is with respect to re-acquisition of its own shares at current market prices?

Mr. Garrett: No, I cannot. But maybe if you watch the newspapers, you will get some ideas in the future not too far off. I mentioned the fully disclosed fraud. Well, there you might have it in a properly presented case. But first you have got to decide that for controlling stockholders to cause the corporation to buy up, use its own money and its own credit, and to buy up enough shares to further enhance the position of that controlling stockholder to the detriment of the non-exchange stockholders who are left with an unlisted or perhaps not even '34 Act registered, if you have gotten down below 300 people you can delist under the Exchange Act.

If you decide it is wrong, how do you reach it under the securities laws if the whole thing is fully explained in the offered material? There you have got to see whether or not our laws of fully disclosed fraud apply but you have to agree whether the case is fully disclosed to begin with.

Question: Suppose an inexperienced director is clearly over his head in dealing with highly complex financial matters. If he stays on the board, is he liable for fraud he innocently fails to detect?

Mr. Garrett: I don't think so if he makes an adequate showing of diligence. I suppose, in measuring other people in other jobs, there is a degree of disability that makes it negligence or careless for you even to undertake a job. So I suppose you might be dumb enough and inexperienced enough so that you have no business being on the board, and that is your fault. But assuming we haven't gone quite that far, I think that certainly we and the law are not trying to penalize people who are honestly trying to do the best they can.

Question: May a nominated director be held liable before he is actually installed as a director?

Mr. Garrett: Not in general under what I group as the fraud provisions. It is true in the public offering and registration statement context that expressly includes persons who are named with their consent about to become directors, and they are stuck with Section 11.

Question: Should a member of an audit committee of a board of directors be held to a higher standard of investigation of the activities of the corporation than just the regular outside member of the board?

Mr. Garrett: Well, certainly not of all activities. I suppose by undertaking the duty he might be held for not having learned things about the financial procedures and statements of the company that an ordinary director wouldn't be supposed to know. It's sort of a sad thing to contemplate. We are not setting them up to be sitting ducks, held to a higher standard for him to do a good job. But I suppose, like anything else, if you take a job and don't do it with reasonable care, you could be held responsible for it.

The SEC Requirements:

The Corporate Viewpoint

PART ONE

Richard T. Murphy, Jr.

Arthur D. Little, Inc.

Mr. Murphy is Vice President, Secretary, and General Counsel of Arthur D. Little, Inc. He is also an officer and director of Arthur D. Little International, Inc. He has been responsible for dealing with a wide range of corporate legal problems involving the operations of the company domestically and in several overseas locations. He is also responsible for the legal affairs of the domestic and foreign subsidiaries of the company and has been active in a number of cases involving the application of law to management and economic development problems.

Mr. Murphy is also a Senior Lecturer in Law at the Sloan School of Industrial Management, Massachusetts Institute of Technology.

You now have before you three lawyers who are also corporate secretaries, at least two of whom, my colleagues on the panel from Monsanto and Con Ed, are most prominent indeed. They bring a wealth of experience in years and in the complexity and significance of the problems they have faced and solved. Both gentlemen are general counsel and secretary of major American corporations, both have been or are director and president of the American Society of Corporate Secretaries or its regional components.

As a comparative newcomer to the ranks of corporate secretaries, I have always found it difficult to answer the question: "What do you do?" The statutory definition is quite simple; just look at the by-laws of your corporation or the state incorporation statutes. But what a corporate secretary really does, it seems to me speaking from my wealth of three years of experience, is very much influenced by the chairman of his board and the particular kind of corporation that he works for. It is the dynamics of the entity that he is involved in that he begins to understand.

The secretary, therefore, has a unique opportunity to observe his board and understand how it operates, and to see the problems that its members face and to help them try to solve them. And right at the top of that list, of course, is the so-called SEC regulations. Now, Mr. Garrett has just told us that directors must do their job well and that there are a whole host of traditional and some very new liabilities which lurk in the wings if they don't do their job well. At the same time he tells us that we as of this date at least cannot expect any meaningful guidelines from his office.

Now, while this may make a few cheer, as some of you did, and warm the heart of Byron Smith, who packed up and left having heard that welcome announcement, it still leaves us with what the common law lawyers have always referred to as precedent, which is a way of saying that you read history, you consider the matter carefully, you do what you think is right, and if you are wrong, we will tell you about it later on. And the Commission has been struggling with this problem and as late as last August Commissioner Summer was telling us that they are still coming, but are a little difficult. He referred to them in a speech at the American Bar Association as a little bit of prophecy mixed with legal analysis.

Well, Mr. Garrett has told us they have given up that fight, we can't expect them at all. But I think our panelists will have something helpful to say about this, we hope.

including on one occasion a single memorandum on a single transaction that was over 400 pages in length. That is known in the trade as snowing the board and is equivalent to sending out no information at all. Busy directors cannot be expected to read and absorb that much information. If the subject is a technical one, the first draft should probably be prepared by the company's scientists and technicians and will be incomprehensible to the ordinary director. Later drafts can be worked up among the technicians and your more literate corporate secretary.

Incidentally, the discipline of preparing the memorandum occasionally tells management that the project really isn't yet ready for the board. As one of my old law school professors used to say, "If you can't write it, you don't understand it." In the preparation of the agenda the secretary should constantly try to put himself in the position of an outside director: intelligent, hard working, well meaning, sound of judgment, but not an expert in nuclear physics or petrochemical engineering. It is hard and demanding work to present technical matters in a simple, balanced, and comprehensive manner to a board composed of businessmen, lawyers, bankers, and other non-scientific directors.

In addition to the items which require specific action, the agenda should in my view include financial statements appropriate to your business, usually a comparative income statement, and a balance sheet. But if you include only the financial statements, you will remind me of those very cluttered children's cartoons that said at the bottom, "Can you find nine animals in the above picture?" Usually as a child I could find only seven or eight of the animals, but seldom all nine. With the financial statements, you should include some explanatory analysis in words to tell the board member who reads as he runs what hidden meaning is buried in line 15 of the income statement.

Third, and not everyone agrees with me on this, I believe that the board should adopt specific rules as to what actions require board authorization and what actions are delegated to management. Despite the disagreement of my friends who say I may be tying management's hands, I don't think a management should be free to decide whether or not to take a particular item to the board. For example, how large should a capital item be to require board approval, or a lease, or a contract to sell real estate, or a salary increase? How large should a cost overrun be before it has to come back to the board?

I suggest clear predetermined rules on these matters approved by your board. This is a complex area in which the rules should be tailored to fit your particular company.

Fourth, decide how frequently your board should meet. For most companies, I believe regular monthly meetings are advisable. Some companies may even need more frequent meetings. But when I hear of a board that meets quarterly, I suspect it is a rubber stamp or it is a board of a relatively inactive business. Special items of business, such as debt or equity financings or acquisitions, may require special meetings. The chairman or the secretary should not hesitate to advise the board in writing of important or interesting developments between meetings. A few examples of mailings that we have done recently involve developments in labor negotiations, an important regulatory decision, a forthcoming important press release that the company is about to put out, and even not too long ago a significant policy speech by a Commissioner of the SEC.

Fifth, give the board members a chance to make suggestions. They are smart or they wouldn't be on your board. So we ought to just listen once in a while. This obviously includes the opportunity to ask questions and to have free discussion at board meetings, as Mr. Magee was advocating today. In addition, we recently held a special evening board meeting to discuss one subject only, whether management was doing a good job in informing our board, what the board was getting that was not useful to the performance of its job, and what it was lacking that would be more useful. It was the liveliest and most productive meeting we have had in years and led to a number of suggestions which we adopted with enthusiasm.

I remember reading in the book *The Wreck of the Penn Central* the mournful commentary of one director that as a director he received a packet of information each month, but that a list of purchases of rolling stock really had not informed him of the company's financial situation. Maybe if he had been asked an earlier question whether he was getting the kind of information he wanted, he would have made a valuable contribution. Parenthetically, I find that directors frequently are hesitant to make suggestions for changes. The invitation to them to tell you what they understand and what they don't understand, what they are not getting that would be helpful to them, brings forth a torrent that has been penned up inside of them sometimes for years.

Sixth, and this has probably been discussed at the conference, I would strongly urge you to establish committees of the board to examine important aspects of your business. Meetings of such committees give board members the chance to probe into significant complicated problem areas at greater length and in more depth than they ordinarily would receive at board meetings. At a board meeting a director may hesitate to ask five questions in a row about the increase in accounts receivable that he is free to inquire about when the audit committee is in session.

And speaking of audit committees, the SEC has been urging every company to have one. To that I say amen. We have had one since 1940 and I think it is probably one of the two most important committees we have, the other being the finance committee. In addition to the committees I have mentioned, the audit committee and the finance committee, we also have an executive committee, an executive compensation committee, a budget and contracts committee, and a planning and environmental committee. Our committees meet from 12 times a year for the most active committee down to about three meetings a year for the audit committee.

Obviously, the selection of the committees for your company and the frequency of their meetings will depend on your kind of business. But I find it hard to believe that any company doesn't need a finance committee these days to probe into the cash position, accounts receivable, banking arrangements, public financing capabilities, and the like. Obviously, the selection of committee members should make the best use of the particular strengths of your directors. You don't put your environmentalist representative on the finance committee. Committee meetings, of course, precede board meetings and generally report their findings to the board so that the board will have the benefit of the committee's detailed consideration before the board acts. In this area I believe that the General Motors Corporation was an early leader and I commend its practices to your consideration.

Seventh, review with the board from time to time its duties and responsibilities. Responsible directors want to know what the law and the company expect of them. We recently devoted the major portion of a board meeting to this subject and sent out in advance of the meeting a summary of the case law and the statutory law on the subject. You would be surprised how much interest and how many questions and suggestions this meeting generated.

So there we have seven rules that can help your board to do its job. They are easy to state. They are much harder to institute and to carry out and to continue to improve. We could have added a few more. We could have talked about presentations to the board and a variety of other practices, some of which are very useful. We could have made the list 10 or 12 or 15. But the seven items that I have mentioned I think would give you a good start.

I have not spoken today specifically of how we can help the director in new securities issues. Frankly, and I know this is heresy, this is the one area where he has the most assistance in the ordinary case. In the securities issue he is surrounded by certified public accountants, counsel for the company, suspicious and wary underwriters, and able counsel for the underwriters; and even then, through the form of their comments, the staff of the Securities and Exchange Commission. If ever he has professional help in carrying out his duties as a director, it is in the case of new securities issue, and in any event, Mr. Garrett has very ably covered that subject.

It is in the regular business of the company that the director needs the company's help and if the company can help him enough in preparing for regular meetings of the board, he will be better equipped to deal with the problems of the new issues as well as the regular business of the company.

The SEC Requirements:

The Corporate Viewpoint

PART THREE

Edwin J. Putzell, Jr.

Monsanto Company

Edwin J. Putzell, Jr. is a Vice President General Counsel and Corporate Secretary of Monsanto Company.

Mr. Putzell actively participated in drafting the first national legislation on atomic energy (the McMahon Bill), in the development of international aspects of atomic energy control (the Baruch Plan) and served on the American Bar Association's Special Committee on Atomic Energy. Additionally, Mr. Putzell serves on the boards of: Manufacturers Bank & Trust Company of St. Louis; St. Luke's Hospital and the Monsanto Fund, both in St. Louis; Westminster College, Fulton, Mo.; Educational Television Commission (KETC), St. Louis, and the Veterans of Strategic Services.

At Monsanto we have done a couple of things which might be of interest to you.

First, we put together what we call a director's manual, about as comprehensive a set of documents as a director could hope to have with respect to the corporation. This, of course, has particular emphasis for the outside director. We start with a charter and by-laws. We go to what I call a board charter, which I will explain later. We have a summary of his obligations as a director under the pertinent SEC provisions, the short-swing profits, the 10b-5 situation, the obligations with respect to registration statements, and so forth.

We have personnel lists, the membership of the committees of the board, and we have in it the resolutions by which authority is delegated to the president.

This is a living document. We are right now in the process of updating it because our experience has been that it's been a very helpful tool. Now let me explain the board charter. We recently, acquired a new chief executive officer, and in talking with him shortly after his arrival he asked me what I thought about a certain individual as a prospective outside director. I found this to be just the opportunity I had been looking for and I said, "Well, Jack, I can't answer that question directly. I'd like to know your attitude towards the board and what you expect of board members before I can respond."

He asked what I meant. And I said, "Well, do you want a hip pocket board or do you want one which is going to engage in constructive debate?" Then I went down the line with a half dozen similar questions which obviously answered themselves. When we got through, he asked if I'd draft what I thought the Monsanto board charter ought to look like in terms of goals to work toward over the next period of years. We worked on this over a period of several months and came up with a document which is in its first printing.

We have begun to clarify and to relate some of the basic premises that we think are important for the operation of the board of a company like ours as we look into these very uncertain future months and years. This is something that each of you may want to think in terms of. After we got it drafted internally at the staff level, we had it reviewed by our inside directors. There was a fair amount of discussion on it, and then at a meeting of the outside directors with the chief executive officer and the board chairman, we discussed the draft of that document, got their input, and then finally came out with our first edition.

It's an interesting document and I am sure will be polished and improved considerably before it is really worth showing to anybody. There's been talk about evaluations and audits here over the past two days and I happen to be a great believer in the board's evaluation of itself; asking the board on a periodic basis to review what's happened in the corporation over a specified period of time, to review the board's action and inaction, its formal and informal conduct, and to ask itself whether in light of the strategic goals which have been set the board feels it is doing a job.

Professor Koontz has discussed the problems of unhorsing a director who isn't carrying his share of the load. I suspect that if a director were attending meetings physically, but in no other way and not participating, such a frank board self-evaluation might be a useful tool in getting across to him that most everything that went on didn't involve him and that he didn't contribute. I suggested this to another little company on whose board I sit and the result was that one of the directors who attended infrequently and participated very little decided to withdraw as a result of the session.

Further, I think annual audits, what I call due diligence meetings, are important on the board level in all areas of social responsibility. And I needn't go into a lot of detail here, but the EEOC areas that have been mentioned, OSHA, the new pension act, federal pension act, environmental obligations of the company, consumer safety, and so forth.

Here again on the social responsibility end, it would seem to me that an annual audit or due diligence review by the board with the chief executive officer would serve a useful purpose. I'd like also to support the comment on committee work. It seems to me that in a large organization one can pretty well analogize committee work by the board to that of the Congress. Nobody would assume a member of the American Congress to be an expert on all matters that come before it. As you know, they rely very heavily on committee work and men who become experts in the fields which are the responsibilities of given committees.

So it would seem to me to be particularly important in these complicated times; with growing regulation by all governmental bodies, with all kinds of social and political pressures upon us, as well as financial and economic ones, to build on the strengths of special talents within outside directors by putting them on the committees that have been mentioned here and by expecting them to make reports on a regular basis to the board.

If the committee work is well run, the legal exposure of the board members who are not on such committees might be lessened somewhat, if the board committees do their work properly, report properly, and so long also as an individual board member who is not on the committee is not aware of something which countervails the work of the committee.

Lastly, I have the conviction that 99.9 percent of American directors are honest people, diligent, and law-abiding. There is a saying in the law that bad facts make bad law. And I believe that the concern that all of us feel for the environment that is developing as a result of a number of recent actions by the SEC, as well as private actions, results from that one-tenth of one percent of bad apples in the industrial community.

The BarChris case was mentioned earlier and it is sort of a landmark case, but just recently the Mattel Company has been in the press and perhaps you are all aware of what happened. As a result of their issuing misleading statements and non-disclosure of material information, a court ruled that additional outside directors, satisfactory to the SEC, have to be put on the board of the Mattel Corporation; that four outside directors have to review the accounting procedures, controls, financial reports, and the press releases of their company; and that a litigation and claims committee of three outside directors must be established to determine action to be taken concerning claims against officers, directors, and employees of that company.

That was in August. Then, in October, the SEC, having dug a little further into the matter, went back into the courts and sought additional relief. This time they have asked the court to order that a majority of the board be outside and unaffiliated directors, and approved by the Commission and the court; that a majority of the executive committee of the board be outside directors (and likewise approved by the court and the SEC); that a special counsel be appointed to investigate matters with respect to compliance with the federal securities laws and to report his findings to the Commission; that they retain a special auditor to audit the company's financial statements for the years 1971 and '72, and then having done that, that all misstatements and omissions in SEC filings be corrected.

Now, this sounds like a lot of bitter medicine, but I submit to you that when you read the facts on which the litigation is based, you will find it very difficult not to come up with the conclusion that some remedial action of this sort is required. Recently, in a private action brought by three public service groups, the Northrop Corporation entered into a consent judgment. You doubtless will recall that the chief executive officer of that company gave very substantial amounts of corporate funds to the Committee for the Re-election of the President. The consent judgment which was agreed to requires the chief executive to relinquish his post and to repay not only the amount of contributions made to CREEP, but also the expenses incurred by Northrop as a result of the ensuing litigation that it has endured; that four new outside directors be brought onto the board; that the executive committee of the board be revised so that five of its six members become outsiders; and that a nominating committee of the board composed solely of outsiders be established.

And then lastly, of course, there is that large number of so-called tippy cases, or insider trading cases. These have resulted from unfortunate lapses by responsible corporate officials, directors and officers, who for one reason or another have inadvertently disclosed information which wasn't made public generally; with the result, of course, that legal action followed and penalties were incurred.

There is also one case where the company officers weren't involved, but investment bankers passed confidential information out to some of their clients.

Question: I think many directors of corporations these days have been buying their shares back at bargain prices and have had some misgivings. What are your views on this?

Mr. Putzell: Well, I guess I am always simplistic with respect to the non-rigid statutory provisions of the law, sort of like Section 11 registration statement problems under the '33 act that were referred to. When you are talking about negligence, when you are talking about due care, business judgment, prudent man, and all these things, you are talking to me about fairness and equity and common sense. And this is one reason why I was so pleased that Garrett didn't come out with some rigid set of rules.

So much business conduct has to operate within the spectrum of what I call business judgment. There is no one finite point of rightness where everything else is wrong. There's a range of judgments involved. And as long as people operate within that range of judgment that doesn't offend common sense, morality, and ethics, it seems to me that he should not be held responsible. On the other hand, if a person's sense of fairness is offended by what's been done, then I guess he deserves to be dealt with.

And so in the case of rebuying one's own stock, I guess all of us here at times like this, when the market is selling usually below book value, stock selling for below book value, or a multiple that is way off the traditional levels, the temptation is to buy it back. And I would think that one ought to ask himself what his motives are. It is clear to me that if it is true that Mary Welles is doing this for her own personal aggrandizement rather than for other legitimate business or stockholder reasons, there could be some slight offense to me and to others, I guess, with respect to that transaction.

There are, of course, very good business reasons for buying one's stock back. It can be the best way in the world to make money for your stockholders in a given situation. And in the absence of personal motive, either on behalf of the individual who is doing it or some other group, I should think that if it doesn't affect someone's sense of what is right, it ought to be perfectly permissible. And, as Garrett said, there are no laws against it.

Now, he implied to me as I listened to him that the Commission is getting ready to go after this situation. They have already put out press releases, you know, frowning at what is going on, and then the court didn't issue the injunction, so apparently if I can read between the lines in what he said, they are getting ready to test this question about a fully disclosed fraud and it is going to be a question for the trier of fact, probably the judge in this case rather than the jury, as to in his opinion the public was taken advantage of, stockholders whose shares were being sought were being taken advantage of for the aggrandizement of the person who controls the corporation. Huge amounts of American stocks of publicly owned companies are in the hands of street names, registered in street names; broker names. The Williams Act requirements for disclosure when a group acquires five percent or more of the stock of a company, as I recall it, calls for notice to be filed and published within 10 days of an action. It is nice to say we want to encourage investment in American industry by foreign entities, but I have a little concern about the way in which it is accomplished.

Mr. Murphy: I have a question which was addressed to me and it says, "What general and specific duties does a corporate secretary have that cannot be filled by a secretary-clerk?" The secretary-clerk is used in the low case, so I presume that the reference is to a person qualified to take notes at a meeting and to record them. As a matter of fact, in the Commonwealth of Massachusetts we don't refer in our statutes to a secretary, we refer to a clerk. He is called the clerk, he is a statutory officer, one of three required under our laws for the establishment of a corporation. And if that is the kind of secretary you mean, I don't see any difference.

But if what you mean is the note taker, well, then, quite clearly I think the comments that Walter had about the functions of a secretary, whether he be called secretary, corporate secretary, or clerk, go well beyond that. He is the official repository of all the company's records. His ability to seal documents and to sign them and to certify them is a significantly responsible act upon which much of the company's activities revolve. And in most other corporations, of course, he has a whole line of duties, either prescribed in the by-laws or undertaken, which are of a fairly high level.

Question: Mr. Morris, what would be helpful in making more active a board of what was once a "one-man organization" and still bear some philosophic resemblance?

Mr. Morris: It depends on your business, whether it is really a smaller simpler business or whether it has now prospered and grown more complex. If it has prospered and grown more complex, I think it's probably gotten beyond its founder's ability to manage it, and I think he needs the guidance of some outsiders. I am firmly prejudiced against the boards that are heavily inside. If one has a strong chief executive, and most companies that prosper have a strong chief executive, it usually ill-behooves the senior vice president to disagree with him at the board meeting.

On the other hand, if you are an outside director who is a chairman of Metropolitan Life Insurance Company, you can speak up and ask a question or make a suggestion that is not entirely in line with the chairman's viewpoint. Getting outsiders onto the board brings in fresh new points, brings in inquiring minds, brings in people who have experienced similar problems in their own companies or other companies, and it stimulates this intellectual debate that Mr. Magee so eloquently discussed this morning.

You just don't get that with pure inside directors, especially if you have a very firm chief executive officer.

Is the American Board
of the Eighties
Now Being Tested
in Europe?

Wolfgang Heintzeler

BASF

Dr. Heintzeler is a Member of the Supervisory Board, BASF, manufacturers of chemical specialties and industrial chemical products. After serving in several branches of the German Ministry of Justice (1933–36), he joined the legal department of Badische Anilin & Soda-Fabrik (now BASF Aktiengesellschaft) and in 1952 was appointed to the Board of Executive Directors.

Dr. Heintzeler retired in 1973. He is still a member of the Boards of various other firms and associations as well as of the Boards of Trustees of several Max Planck Institutes. He is also an honorary senator of the High School for Administrative Science, Speyer.

The program of this conference provides that I should give you an answer to the question whether the American company board of the 1980's is now being tested in Europe. When formulating this question, the program chairman did certainly not have in mind the general tendencies of company law in Europe with respect to this structure of company boards but rather the special problem of labor representation on company boards. And by labor representation I mean that workers or union officials become members of the company boards with full responsibility and all rights, including the right to vote.

It has been confirmed by Mr. Abel this morning that this problem does not have any real importance in this country so far, and I am sure most of you would find it hard to imagine one-third or 50 percent or any other percentage of the members of your company boards not being elected by the shareholders, but elected or appointed by union workers. In Europe such labor representation on company boards has become an extremely hot issue. On the surface it looks as if the problem were mainly a matter of human relations within the enterprise. But this impression is not correct.

The average worker in Europe does not care very much for such board representation and he does not expect any remarkable improvement of his own situation to result from it. In fact, it is the unions only, at least in Germany, that demand and even fight for labor representation on boards, and in their fight openly admit that it is not so much an improvement of the workers' lot they are aiming at, but rather the fundamental redistribution of power within human society in favor of the unions. You have heard Mr. Abel this morning and what he said about the reasons why German unions fight for more co-determination, and I don't the least doubt that Mr. Abel has been told by his German union colleagues what he told us this morning.

And there is also very little doubt that at the end of the forties this thinking expressed by Mr. Abel had some importance in the minds of German unions. But in the meantime, 30 years have passed by and during the last 10 or 20 years the arguments of the unions in Germany have been absolutely different. I have with me the latest pamphlet published by the top union organization in Germany, a pamphlet which serves their purposes in their fight for more co-determination. It was published three months ago and there is not one word in it of what Mr. Abel said this morning, but there are other things mentioned that talk about redistribution of power. It says that the predominance of capital should be destroyed and it says that the system of a market economy does not exist any more except in the minds of some highly paid lobbyists who are still in favor of an old fashioned market economy system.

It was in the British occupation zone of post-war Western Germany that labor representation on company boards was practiced for the first time in history, and for many years after 1945 this has been an issue within the Federal Republic of Germany only. In recent years, however, due mainly to the intense propaganda of German unions among their fellow unions in other European countries, the demand for workers' representation on company boards has been raised. In Denmark, Sweden, and Norway, laws to this effect already provide for a minority representation of workers on company boards; and in Holland a law has come into effect giving labor and shareholders almost equal representation on the boards.

In Britain the newly elected Labor Government seems to contemplate the introduction of some form of worker representation on British company boards. To repeat, 30 years ago it was introduced by the British in our country. In France, it is likely that in one way or the other the government will have to realize deGaulle's idea of participation. Finally, I should mention that the European Parliament (which is not yet a full-scale parliament, but it is called that way) has quite recently adopted a recommendation (which is not yet European law) to the effect that companies ruled by the future European law should have a board composed of three factions of equal strength: one-third to be elected by the shareholders, one-third to be elected by labor, and the remaining third representing the public interest to be jointly nominated by the two other groups.

In Europe things are moving rapidly and this would seem to justify my going into more detail in presenting the situation to you. Here I should like to ask your permission to concentrate in the following on the developments in my country, not only because the problem originated there, but also because the fight over the issue of how far labor representation on company boards should go has deeply stirred public opinion in Western Germany for many years. And the literature written about co-determination in Europe would fill the whole of a university library by now, which means that in explaining the problem to you I have to simplify it and perhaps sometimes I have to oversimplify things a little bit; otherwise, it would be impossible to give you a presentation within the time available.

So far I have used the term "board" without defining it, and in doing so I have probably given you the impression our board system is equal to that prevailing in your country. And this impression must now be corrected before I can continue. For decades limited companies in Germany do not have one board only, but must have two boards which are clearly distinguished one from the other. Board No. 1 is the so-called supervisory board and the second board is the board of executive directors.

No one is allowed to be a member of both boards at the same time. The business of the company is conducted by the board of executive directors, and membership of that board is a full-time job. Membership in the supervisory board is not a full-time job since this board meets only sporadically. The supervisory board, however, is much more than its name indicates. It is, of course, expected to supervise the activities of the board of executive directors, but the real importance of the supervisory board results from the fact that this body elects the members of the board of executive directors.

Therefore, the composition of the supervisory board has a decisive effect upon the composition of the board of executive directors, and for this reason labor representation on the supervisory board and the relative strength of such representation has become the central issue of co-determination at the corporate level. In effect, the fight about the composition of the supervisory board of German corporations is a fight about two fundamental questions: who rules the companies and who rules the economy of the country.

Before co-determination came up, the members of supervisory boards were elected by the shareholders and by the shareholders only. For more than two decades now, however, part of the supervisory board members have been elected by labor and such co-determination is practiced in two different forms for more than 20 years. In the coal and steel companies of the Ruhr District, labor has a 50 percent representation on the supervisory board. In all other companies, including the industrial companies, insurance companies, banks, and so on, labor has a one-third representation.

This is the present state of affairs based on the law now in force, and I shall now cover the following three questions: How this situation has developed historically; second, which are the merits or the weak points of the two co-determination systems; and third, what changes are envisioned.

As I mentioned, until the end of World War II the supervisory board members were elected by the shareholders only. Prior to the year 1951, the shareholders' meeting elected the supervisory board, and the supervisory board appointed the members of the board of executive directors.

During the period of occupation after the war, the German unions developed a new concept for the composition of the supervisory board which up to then had been representing the shareholders only. According to this new concept shareholders and labor were to have equal representation on the supervisory board, thus giving labor a 50 percent share in electing the board of executive directors; and with the assistance of the British authorities, the German unions succeeded in putting this concept into practice in the coal and steel companies of the Ruhr District.

And from that time onward, the supervisory board of the coal and steel company in the Ruhr had to be composed as follows: assuming the total number of members of the supervisory board is 15, seven members are elected by the shareholders, seven members are jointly nominated by the union and the works council of the company concerned, and the two seven-member groups each agree on the 15th member.

After the occupation period had come to an end, the newly formed legislative body of the Federal Republic of Germany considered the problem of co-determination within the coal and steel industry as it had been evolved. After having studied the system and its effects, the majority of the legislative bodies were not prepared to transform the principle of co-determination into German law. The unions, however, by threatening to provoke a general strike, compelled the German legislators in '51 to enact a special law for the coal and steel industry, giving legal effect to the system of co-determination already described.

This tremendous success, achieved in a rather undemocratic manner, did not satisfy the unions at all. Their aim was to extend this new system to all companies in Germany or at least to all larger companies. This time, however, German legislative bodies did not again yield to union pressure and in 1952 they enacted a law giving labor a one-third representation on the supervisory boards of all German corporations outside the coal and steel industry. Practically speaking, this means, that out of 15 members of the supervisory board, 10 members are elected by the shareholders and five are elected by the company's employees and workers by equal, general, direct, and secret ballot. No direct influence on the nomination of the five labor representatives is given to the unions or the works council but, of course, the unions' indirect influence on such nominations is quite considerable.

I am aware that I now used the words "works council" for the second time and probably it doesn't mean very much to you because, as far as I know, it doesn't exist in this country under this name. A works council is an institution which has existed in German companies since 1921, and it means that the workers and the employees of each plant, not the enterprise or corporation, have to elect every two or three years a body of workers and employees representing them in the daily discussions with management about problems directly affecting workers and employees.

German industrialists and a large part of the German public consider the system of co-determination, as practiced since '52 outside the coal and steel industry, as a good solution, and I agree with it. On the one hand, this system contributes considerably to social peace while on the other hand it is still compatible with an economic system based on free enterprise, private profit, competition, and collective bargaining.

The fact that on the supervisory board freely elected labor representatives take an active part in dealing with all the affairs of importance to the enterprise guarantees that in important decisions human aspects will not be neglected. This one-third representation has also contributed considerably to the removal of the atmosphere of distrust which has, as an outcome of Marxist influences, for a long time infected relations between employers and employees in our country. In most cases, the employees of an enterprise elect their representatives on the supervisory board, persons who are employed in the same enterprise. In general, these members are loyally fulfilling their duties toward the enterprise. In most cases, the attitude of the shareholders' representatives on the supervisory board is also governed by the spirit of loyalty to their enterprise, their aim being to reach decisions if at all possible unanimously.

And during the more than 20 years in which I have been a member of the executive board of our company, I can't remember any case where it was impossible to reach a unanimous decision. Shareholders' representatives endeavored always to negotiate so long until the possibility of a unanimous decision with the shareholders' representatives had been reached.

Naturally, the unions criticize the fact that under the one-third/two-thirds system the employees are placed in a minority position, but this criticism can be met.

Outside the supervisory board, the influence of labor on the enterprise is much stronger than the influence of capital, given the daily presence of the works council (which I have to explain and to which no counterpart exists on the side of the shareholders) and given the power of the unions which in our country are highly centralized organizations. The unions in our country now represent the most powerful political institution. There are some smaller unions besides the one big powerful centralized union organization, but politically it is only one organization which is really of importance. The shareholders majority on the supervisory board serves to balance labor's preponderance outside and thus creates a balance of power in the enterprise as a whole.

In contrast to this positive attitude towards the one-third representation of labor, German businessmen are most decidedly opposed to the model of 50 percent co-determination and they are still more opposed to the idea strongly advocated by the unions that this coal and steel model should now be extended to all companies employing more than 2,000 persons. The reasons for such opposition are as follows.

Under the coal and steel system, labor representatives on the supervisory board are not elected by the workers of the enterprise, but are appointed under the unions' dominating influence. Consequently, labor representatives under the coal and steel system consider themselves rather as the unions' prolonged arm than as representatives of the employees of the individual enterprise. And if a labor representative under the coal and steel system wants to be re-elected after his term has passed, then it is much more important for him not to have lost the favor of the unions than to have gained the sympathy of his fellows within the enterprise.

Equal representation on the supervisory board splits up the supervisory board into two opposing factions, the capital faction and the union faction. And if agreement between these two factions cannot be reached, the 15th member, who is supposed to make the decision, often does not see fit to take responsibility alone. This was one of the unanimous findings of a government commission. In spite of the fact that the nine professors came from various political parties and groups, they reached a unanimous decision that the neutral 15th member is mostly not able to take the responsibility alone. Consequently, it often happens that important decisions are either delayed to the detriment of the enterprise or are made possible only by concessions to the unions, which is the most dangerous aspect of the thing.

Equal representation on supervisory boards of capital and labor will sooner or later be followed by equal representation on the board of executive directors. This body will thus be deprived of its ability to act as a homogenous team responsible for the conduct of the business. Moreover, two factions within the board of executive directors will mean a split through all levels of the enterprise, so that in effect two careers are created, one characterized by performance, the other by union membership. The coal and steel model means that the labor representatives with the help of the 15th member can place the shareholders' representatives in a minority position and in effect this model may, therefore, lead sometimes to an indirect expropriation of the shareholders.

The coal and steel model, though it seductively appears to offer parity of capital and labor, actually means a stronger disparity of capital and labor in the enterprise as a whole. I explain that because outside the supervisory board the influence of labor is much stronger than the influence of capital. Evidently, the coal and steel model is not compatible with a system of collective bargaining. How could such bargaining be conducted freely if the unions have a 50 percent say in the companies with which they bargain and if, as it happened, managers of such companies run the risk of putting at stake periodic renewal of their nomination as a board member by arousing the unions' anger in the process of bargaining?

The coal and steel system gives the unions the possibility of gaining central control over the enterprises. Thus, it will sooner or later destroy competition as one of the most important basic principles of a free market economy, and it will subordinate consumers' interest to the group interest of labor as seen by the unions. An enterprise in which labor considerations are more important than normal economic considerations, such as profitability, will no longer be able to compete in a market economy, either on a national or international level.

And if, as a result of an extension of the coal and steel co-determination, the highly centralized union system were to become the dominant factor in the economy, then the economic as well as the political system would slowly, but inevitably, change into syndicalism, which means a model of things in which the unions are a predominant factor, and there would be nothing and nobody to control the enormous concentration that is put into the hands of the unions.

I now come to my question No. 3. Several years ago the German unions started a most powerful campaign in order to achieve the extension of the coal and steel co-determination to all companies employing more than 2,000 persons. What are their chances? Since 1969 we have had a coalition government. I now have to describe the political scene, otherwise I am afraid you can't understand the situation.

We had a coalition government formed by the big Social Democratic Party, the party of Brandt and now of Helmut Schmidt, and the small Free Democratic Party, which jointly have a narrow majority in our parliament. The Social Democratic Party clearly takes sides with the unions in advocating an extension of the coal and steel model to all bigger enterprises. The Free Democrats defined their attitude towards co-determination during a party congress in fall, 1971, and on that occasion added a new feature to the co-determination discussion by demanding a separate representation for the so-called high level employees on the supervisory board.

That party congress of the so-called Liberal Party disclosed that this party had moved very far to the left. Strong groups within the party advocated co-determination models which definitely put shareholders into a minority position on the supervisory board and at last the congress, by the majority of one vote, accepted the following model.

Six out of the twelve members of the supervisory board are to be elected by the shareholders, four members are to be elected by lower level employees, and two members by high level employees. This model means that the shareholders wouldn't have a majority position any longer, but they would not be in the minority position. Some of the initiators of this model were of the opinion that it was very likely that the two representatives of high level employees would always vote with the shareholders' representatives, thus ensuring the shareholders' majority position.

But many people, including myself, are highly doubtful as to whether this speculation is correct. If this model became law, the practical effect would largely depend on the question on how the term "high level employees" is to be defined, and if it is defined as a very large group, then it cannot be taken for granted at all that the representatives of the high level employees would in all or most cases vote with the shareholders' representatives. Thus, the position of the two coalition parties has been clear and for many, many months the Social Democrats and the Free Democrats kept trying in secret negotiations to find a compromise on co-determination.

At last in January of this year it was announced that agreement had been reached and some weeks later the government submitted to parliament a draft of the law based on that agreement. This complicated model presents itself as follows: out of the 20 members of the supervisory board, 10 should be elected by the shareholders' meeting, the other 10 members representing labor should be elected indirectly by a group of electors which are nominated by the employees and the workers. Three out of the ten labor members should be union representatives and one of this group should be a high level employee. That is a concession to the liberals. But the latter was not to be elected by the high level employees as a group, but indirectly in the same way as the rest of the labor representatives; and the group of high level employees would have only a weak right to nominate.

A neutral member No. 21 is not provided and this, of course, raises the question how can a decision be reached if the two groups of 10 members each cannot agree. The impracticability of this draft can be seen from the stipulations which try to take care of the situation of a deadlock between the two groups.

I may mention that there is no provision for the chairman of the supervisory board to have the deciding vote; and there is no provision that the chairman of the supervisory board should always be taken from the representatives of the shareholders. The draft of the law says that the two groups should agree on the chairman and the deputy chairman and if they cannot agree, then each group names one man and these two men alternate as chairman and deputy chairman. And if they cannot agree who is first chairman of the supervisory board, then the question has to be decided by lot.

Well, these are some examples from which you will agree with me that this law cannot be practicable and that if it should be enacted, it would certainly make impossible businesslike decisions within the company and it would certainly not be to the advantage of the economy of our country.

Now, finally enough, this compromise model which has been developed by the two coalition parties, though it is very close to the unions' demand, is sharply criticized by everybody, including the unions. The unions mainly criticize this compromise because of the fact that out of the 10 labor representatives, one has to be a high level employee. Although the election procedure has the effect that no high level employee has a chance to become a member of the supervisory board unless he finds the approval of the unions, the unions still dislike even the slightest possibility that one of the ten labor representatives may not be subject to union discipline and may escape union control.

As I mentioned, business in Germany holds that this coalition model will be totally impractical, that it will subject all enterprises to more or less total union control, and that it will mark the end of the market economy and lead to a system whereby the unions dominate the economy and perhaps the state. Although the coalition parties both affirm that their model will now become law, the legislative procedure may prove that the devil is to be found in its details and the last few months have shown that this procedure moves very slowly and that detailed questions are still debated between the two parties.

Now, I know that the present German Chancellor, Mr. Helmut Schmidt, when he was in the United States, made a public statement in which he said that certainly the coalition model would become law within the year of 1975 which, considering the fact that his party has not a majority in the parliament and has to have the support of the Liberals in order to enact the law, it remains to be seen what will happen during the present legislative sessions. We have had public hearings in parliament and the representatives of German business have clearly expressed their misgivings and their fears with respect to the draft of this law.

The question now is: what would happen if the Christian Democrats, now the biggest opposition party, and which lacks only a few votes in order to win the majority, should return to power? There is very little doubt that they would enact a co-determination law on the basis of a 50-50 representation of capital and labor on the supervisory board.

The Christian Democratic Party Congress in November, 1973, agreed on the following co-determination model as part of the party's program. According to this, only party shareholders and labor nominate one half each of the members of the supervisory board, and in cases of dissent between the two groups of equal strength, the chairman of the supervisory board would have the deciding vote. The chairman of the supervisory board would be elected by a two-thirds majority of the board; but if such majority cannot be reached, the chairman should be elected by the shareholders' meeting.

By this provision, the Christian Democratic model looks a little bit better than the present model of the coalition government, but still it shows a rather curious mixture of parity in figures and disparity in substance and it remains to be seen whether the Christian Democrats, if and when they are returned to power, will have the political strength to sustain the elements of disparity in substance contained in their model.

In concluding, I would like to turn to the question of whether there would be anything attractive in our European experiences for this country. The only European country in which a real test of labor participation has been made over a period of time long enough to yield results is Western Germany, and with respect to the 50 percent participation of labor, the results of our 20 year tests are, as I hope to have made you realize, clearly negative, and it is easy to foresee that after an extension of the system to all bigger companies, even though perhaps in a slightly modified form, test results would be even more negative.

If such 50 percent participation should indeed be put to the test in all big companies during the remaining years of the 1970's, you may at the beginning of the 1980's discover an economy in Western Germany from which all essential elements of free enterprise have disappeared, and in which perhaps a number of union officials have become happier, but certainly not individual workers. With respect to the one-third labor participation on company boards, I would say again that the results of our 20 years test are encouraging. But always keeping in mind the conditions of our country, which had to overcome a complete breakdown after a disastrous war and which also had a long Marxist tradition among its workers.

I feel unable, however, to answer the question whether this one-third system can be recommended as an article for export to other countries, especially to such countries where the majority of workers and employees has never opposed in principle the system of free enterprise as such, and where other methods of integrating workers and employees into the country's social system have been developed and practiced with great success.

Question: Dr. Heintzeler, where does co-determination rank on the priority list of workers' wishes?

Dr. Heintzeler: Results of investigations show clearly that the workers do not care much about co-determination. They are much more interested in wages and salaries, vacation, and good human relations; co-determination is deep down on the priority list. This is especially true, and it is astonishing, with respect to the coal and steel companies, perhaps for the reason that there the labor representatives on the supervisory board are not elected directly by the workers, but are appointed by the unions and the works council. So that the individual worker in most cases doesn't know who the representative is on the supervisory board.

Question: How far has share ownership by these workers been developed in Germany? Do you consider this share ownership of workers as an alternate solution to co-determination?

Dr. Heintzeler: Well, for many years it was a widespread feeling that share ownership of workers might be an alternative to integrate the workers into the social, economic, and political system. Our own company, for the last 15 years, at the end of the year, always offers the workers and employees some shares at a reduced rate. Apparently due to these endeavors the number of shareholders in our company has been considerably increased.

I think when the stock exchange started to work again about 1952 and 1953, we may have had 500,000 shareholders in Western Germany, and this figure increased to about four and a half million now. But we have come to a point where this development stopped, mainly due to the fact that the stock exchange is in a desperate condition. I think it is not much different from this country, and it is very difficult to induce a worker now to invest his money in shares of the company.

So I feel that practically speaking share ownership of workers has not yet been sufficiently developed in our country in order to be an alternative to co-determination.

Question: Have coal and steel profits in Germany suffered as a result of the 50-50 board and what is the comparison of coal and steel rates of return on investment as compared with other industries?

Dr. Heintzeler: Well, the question is rather simple to answer with respect to coal. The conditions in the coal industry were so terrible about six or eight years ago that the government had to make a merger of all the coal companies into one unified coal company which, of course, has a very strong position on the market. And co-determination within this unified coal company has been further developed with a result that most people look at the coal company no more as a private company, but as a sort of nationalized enterprise.

With respect to steel, I think profits have not been bad, mainly due to the fact that prices have grown more than in other industries. Whether this may be due to the fact that the steel companies had all the same control agency in the form of the union must be left open, but certainly I think co-determination has contributed to the increase of prices for steel at least in some years, thus preventing a decrease of profits.

Appendixes

Questions to Be Asked Concerning Total Board Effectiveness

Harold Koontz
University of California, Los Angeles

A. The Board's Role in Management

1. Does the board have an understanding of whom it represents?
2. Does the board have an awareness of the role of managers?
3. Does the board have an awareness of the legal requirements of the corporation under various laws and, where the board is uncertain, is legal counsel readily available and used?
4. Is the board as a whole and each member of it clearly aware of the ethical (even though not illegal) standards the community expects of the board?
5. Is the board's area of reserved decision-making authority carefully clarified so that it and operating officers know what types of policies, programs, appointments, and other matters must be submitted to it for final decision?
6. Does the chief executive officer and his key subordinates know on what areas the board wishes information of plans and programs, even where the decision authority has been delegated by the board?
7. Does the board meddle in operating matters not within its provinces?
8. Does the chairman or president often make decisions within the board's reserved scope of authority, and when he does, does he explain the reasons for so doing and ask for board ratification of his decision?
9. When board committees are used to handle a portion of a board's responsibilities, are the committees' powers clearly spelled out and are committee decisions or recommendations reported for board information or action?
10. Does the board act only as a group of staff specialists to advise the chairman or president?
11. Does the board as a whole understand its role as the top manager of the company?

B. Areas of Board Decision Making

1. Does the board reserve for itself final decision in the following matters:
   a. Determination of overall company objectives?

    b. *Major* policies (not day-to-day decisions) with respect to new products, research and development, marketing approaches, pricing, procurement of funds, cash utilization, dividend policy, personnel, executive compensation and development, and public relations?

    c. Basic nature and form of company organization structure?

    d. Approval of selection of top key personnel?

    e. Top management compensation?

    f. Summary operating and capital budgets?

    g. Major corporate plans and commitments and has "major" been defined (usually in terms of those matters which substantially affect the future growth of the company)?

    h. Appointment of outside auditors and general legal counsel?

    i. Terms and conditions on which outsiders legally represent the company?

    j. Matters where stockholders' action is required?

2. In the decision areas reserved to it, does the board recognize, and insist on receiving from operating executives, adequate staff counsel and proposals for needed action?

3. Does the board become so involved in immediate problems and decisions that it overlooks the long range impact of current decisions?

4. Does the board become so entrenched in company affairs that it tends to overlook the fact that long-range profitability and success requires being aware of and responsive to the external environment in all its aspects—technological, economic, social, political, and ethical?

5. Does the board regularly receive carefully developed income and cash flow forecasts and satisfy itself on the assumptions utilized?

C. How A Board Manages

1. Does the board insist on adequately researched and analyzed recommendations (with both advantages and disadvantages noted) being submitted to it on matters where it is called upon to make a decision?

2. Is the information presented to the board appropriate to guide it in its basic function as the top management group—planning, organizing, staffing, directing, and controlling?

3. Is the information presented to the board understandable to members without requiring undue effort on their part?

4. Is the board, in fact, comprised of members who can and will speak freely on issues presented to it?

5. Does the board consciously or unconsciously insist on reaching a unanimous decision on matters, even if this may mean a compromise at the least common denominator?

6. Does the board ferret out the critical or limiting factor in decision questions before it?

D.   Making Board Operation Effective

1.   Is the chairman an effective chairman?
2.   Is the board large enough to permit adequate representation of various needed experience and points of view, yet small enough to make free discussion of issues presented to it?
3.   Does the board have enough outside members on it and is it so operated as to provide an "outside look"?
4.   Do insider members unduly dominate the board?
5.   Do insider members, when acting as board members, take a company rather than an operating department, point of view in board deliberations?
6.   Are the board members presented with a clear and complete agenda before each meeting?
7.   Are board members given financial reports, program proposals, studies and recommendations, and other assistance before the meeting far enough in advance so that individual members may have an opportunity to prepare for matters requiring board action?
8.   Where advisable for board education, are board members given occasional pre-meeting briefings, inspection trips, and other means of becoming familiar with the company and its operations?
9.   Are board meetings long enough to allow adequate discussion of issues?
10.   Does the board meet at least ten times per year, or if less frequently, are board committees provided for interim meetings?

E.   The Board Function of Control

1.   After approving major policies, programs, or other matters falling within their decision-making authority, is the board periodically given information as to how well operating managers are performing as compared to plan?
2.   Does the board, or a committee of it, regularly (probably quarterly) review the performance of the company as a whole and, where major divisions justify board attention, the performance of these divisions?
3.   If performance fails to live up to plan, is the board given adequate reasons for failure and an opportunity to see or approve a revised program designed better to attain company objectives?
4.   Is the control information tailored to board needs in terms of board areas of concern, the limitations of board time, and the need for relative ease of understanding?

F.   Assuring Effective Executives

1.   Does the board insist upon the company utilizing an effective program of management by objectives?

2. Are board members given an opportunity to know and evaluate key top executives, other than those on the board?

3. Does the chairman occasionally have key non-board executives attend a portion of the board meeting in order to present matters of special concern to these executives?

4. Does the board assure itself that the company has an effective program of management selection, appraisal and development?

5. Is the board satisfied that managers are being adequately and effectively compensated through salary and other inducements?

6. Does the board assure itself that, to the extent practicable, the company's program of executive bonuses is based, to a significant extent, on performance of *individual* executives?

7. Does the board as a whole and as individuals do what they can to assist the chief executive in carrying out his responsibilities?

G. Assuring An Effective Group of Board Members

1. Who really selects the board? Is that what is desired and in the best interests of the stockholders?

2. Has the board consciously attempted to obtain a spread in age, interests, and points of view among its membership? Is the board "balanced"?

3. Does the membership provide an adequate "outside look," regardless of the number of outside board members?

4. Have provisions been made for retirement of directors?

5. In selecting board members is care taken not to have undue conflicts of interests among members?

6. Do the individual board members respect each other and each other's judgment, even while materially differing in positions on board matters?

7. Is the board so organized and operated as to make individual directors feel they are contributing to the effective and successful management of the company?

8. Are the board members adequately motivated through status, satisfaction of task accomplished, compensation, or other inducements?

Questions for the Individual Board Member to Ask Himself

Harold Koontz
University of California, Los Angeles

A. **My Position as a Director**

1. Why was I selected to be a board member?
2. Why am I serving as a board member?
3. Does my position on the board involve any serious conflict of interest with any other board membership, corporate position, investment, or friendship? Have I disclosed any significant actual or potential conflict of interest to the other board members?
4. Do I understand what decision areas are reserved to the board and what are delegated to operating management?
5. Do I resist meddling in operating areas not the province of the board?
6. Do I have a clear understanding of what my legal and ethical responsibilities are as a board member?
7. If I am an insider with a divisional or functional operating responsibility, do I lay aside the prejudices of my operating position and make decisions as a board member with the entire corporate interest uppermost in my mind?
8. If I am an insider, subordinate to the chairman or president, do I feel I must support their positions on a board matter, even if I believe them to be unwise?
9. Do the corporation minutes accurately reflect the actions of the board? Am I given an opportunity to review these minutes before final approval?
10. Am I willing to put in a reasonable amount of time, interest, and commitment to discharge the responsibilities of a company director?
11. Am I willing to resign, after notice and attempting to obtain desirable changes, if I feel that the board is not being effectively used, if the company is not being well managed, or if the actions being taken are not in the best interests of the stockholders?

B.   How Do I See That The District Is Well Managed?

1. Do I insist on receiving adequate information (on decision area proposals, control and other matters of board concern) so that I may be assured that the company is being effectively managed?
2. When matters are submitted for board action, do I insist on well researched and analyzed recommendations being presented?
3. Am I willing to ask probing, discerning, and even embarrassing questions to assure myself that recommended courses of action have been thoroughly thought through?
4. In a matter before the board, do I attempt to identify the critical factors in a decision and satisfy myself that these have been adequately considered?
5. When I detect that the board has not taken a recent look at such important matters as review of company objectives, management succession and compensation, organization structure, financial marketing and new product plan, have I raised strong questions as to why these and similar matters have been overlooked?

C.   How Do I Help To Make The Board Effective

1. Do I attend meetings regularly?
2. Do I come to board meetings prepared on reports and other information sent me in advance of the meeting?
3. Am I sure the board meets often enough that I am able to discharge my obligations as a board member?
4. On a matter that I feel is important and on which my judgment differs from other board members, do I seek a compromise in order to obtain unanimity even though I believe the compromise to be unsound?
5. Do I feel a sense of commitment to the company and its objectives?
6. Am I willing to give a reasonable amount of assistance to the chief executive and the company outside of board meetings?
7. Do I help in recruiting and evaluating qualified new board members?
8. Do I recognize that, while the board represents the stockholders of the corporation as a whole, the long-range success of the company requires being responsive to the external economic, technological, political, social, and ethical environment in which the corporation operates?